The False Promise of Global Learning

Why education needs boundaries

The False Promise of Global Learning

Why education needs boundaries

Alex Standish

continuum

KH

Continuum International Publishing Group

The Tower Building	80 Maiden Lane
11 York Road	Suite 704
London	New York
SE1 7NX	NY 10038

www.continuumbooks.com

ISBN: HB: 978-1-4411-9839-6
PB: 978-1-4411-5591-7

Library of Congress Cataloging-in-Publication Data
Standish, Alex.
The false promise of global learning : why education needs boundaries/
Alex Standish.
p. cm.
Includes bibliographical references and index.
ISBN-13: 978-1-4411-9839-6 (hardcover : alk. paper)
ISBN-10: 1-4411-9839-3 (hardcover : alk. paper)
ISBN-13: 978-1-4411-5591-7 (pbk. : alk. paper)
ISBN-10: 1-4411-5591-0 (pbk. : alk. paper)
1. Global method of teaching. 2. International education.
3. Education and globalization. 4. Curriculum change. I. Title.
LB1029.G55.S73 2012
371.39–dc23
2012003062

Typeset by Deanta Global Publishing Services, Chennai, India
Printed and bound in the United States of America.

10/20/14

CONTENTS

ACKNOWLEDGMENTS

There are a number of people without whom this project would not have been possible. Firstly, I am grateful to the schools and organizations that opened their doors for me to learn about what they do and the thinking that informs their practice. I would also like to thank all the individuals who gave their time to be interviewed, provided me with a guided tour, or allowed me to observe their class. During these visits I witnessed some dedicated teaching and many enthused children. I applaud the hard work and commitment of these teachers. Gratitude is also due to those individuals and organization who granted permission for the reproduction of materials used herein to illustrate global education.

Although this book offers a critique of the recent trend towards global learning in schools and colleges, I share many common aspirations with the people I met along the way. These include the desire to improve the condition of public (state) schooling in both the US and England, a belief in the importance of teaching children about the world beyond their communities and nations, the view that schools need to do a better job of engaging children in discussion about ethical issues, and also that we should be offering children the best education we possibly can. The analysis provided in this text is written with these aims in mind. The need for distinctions or boundaries in education is here asserted as a necessary path to clarifying the meaning of education as well as which individuals, communities, and institutions are responsible for this task.

I would also like to thank Jennie Bristow, Frank Furedi, Toby Marshall, and Elizabeth Lasch-Quinn for their feedback on my work, Stephen Muffatti for research assistance, as well as David Barker at Continuum for publishing the manuscript. As ever, I am indebted to my wife, Sarah, for her support and love.

LIST OF ILLUSTRATIONS

ABBREVIATIONS

Applicable to the United States

AP	Advanced Placement
CCSSO	Council of Chief State School Officers
CGE	Council for Global Education
NAIS	National Association for Independent Schools
NGA	National Governors Association
NEA	National Education Association
P21	Partnership for 21st Century Skills

Applicable to the United Kingdom

A Level	Advanced Level Examination
CAFOD	Catholic Agency for Overseas Development
CARE	Christian Action Research and Education
CCEA	Council for the Curriculum, Examinations and Assessment
DEA	Development Education Association
DES	Department of Education and Science (1964–92)
DfID	Department for International Development
GCSE	General Certificate in Secondary Education
GNVQ	General National Vocational Qualification
NVQ	National Vocational Qualification
OFSTED	Office for Standards in Education
QCDA	Qualifications and Curriculum Development Agency, formerly the Qualifications and Curriculum Authority (QCA)
RISC	Reading International Solidarity Centre
WEDG	World Education Development Group

Other

EU   European Union
IB   International Baccalaureate
IBO   International Baccalaureate Organization
NGOs   Non-Governmental Organizations
UNESCO   United Nations Educational, Scientific, and
            Cultural Organization
UNICEF   The United Nations Children's Fund
VSO   Voluntary Services Overseas
WWF   World Wildlife Fund

PREFACE

As a geographer I was naturally curious about the expanding movement for global or international education at the beginning of the new millennium. I have dedicated much of my life to advancing the place of geographical knowledge in schools and universities. In the USA geography has poor curricular standing, while in England much geography teaching has moved away from its disciplinary foundations. I imaged that a movement for global/international education would educate children and higher education students about distant places, people, landscapes, and cultures. I hoped that it would be rich in knowledge of history, geography, art, languages, music, biology, politics, and literature. Yet, at the same time I knew, from academic literature and personal experience, that the average child or young person in England and the USA knows less about these areas of knowledge than those of previous generations, a situation that is getting worse not better. How could it be that global/international education was all the rage at the same time that schools and universities were failing to successfully educate their charges about the world? This is the challenge I explore in this book. The answer I found is that contemporary global and international education initiatives often have less to do with educating about the world and more to do with breaking down the boundaries between education and noneducational endeavors, such as training, political activism, and therapy. The 'global' approach seeks to revise the very meaning and purpose of education, inadvertently undermining its foundations in subject knowledge.

Alex Standish, 2012

FOREWORD

Globalization is one of those terms the meaning of which is represented as self-evident. Since the 1980s, expressions like the "forces of globalization" are used to account for virtually every dimension of human experience. Businessmen, citizens, and students are constantly exhorted to "think global" and are lectured about the need to look beyond the confines of their nation. The narrative of globalization invariably communicates the idea of ceaseless change. Policy documents constantly inform the public that a globalized society is somehow qualitatively different from the previous stages of human existence. On closer inspection what the various claims about globalization represent are the sentiment of uncertainty, impermanence, and estrangement from the legacy of the past.

It is useful to recall that back in 1930, when this term was invented, it was educators who first wrote about globalization. Since pedagogy has become so overwhelmed by the idea of ceaseless change it is not surprising that it has embraced this concept. Since the nineteenth century groups of educational theorists have claimed that so-called traditional education could not prepare young people for a constantly changing world. With the arrival of the term globalization these educators could express their obsession with novelty through a widely understood idiom. The emergence of so-called global education was justified on the ground that schools need to adopt its wisdom if young people are to keep up with the new reality of an ever changing internationally connected world.

The advocacy of global education invariably expresses the problem that contemporary society has in endowing experience with meaning. The phenomenon often described as the "crisis of education" symbolizes a much wider problem, which is the difficulty that modern society has in giving the kind of meaningful account of itself that can serve as the cornerstone for authoritative adult behaviour. In such circumstances it is tempting to blame the intellectual legacy underpinning classical western education than to confront the problem that educators have in transmitting it. Global education is one of a number of innovations developed to bypass the problem of meaning. By reinterpreting education as a set of skills and competencies necessary to deal with a changing world, global education avoids the challenge of engaging with an academic, intellectually challenging, and subject-based curriculum.

As Alex Standish explains, global education has little to do with education. It is policy-driven and is motivated by an agenda that is external to the problems that have emerged in the classroom. Yes, we want our children to transcend the parochial context of their life. And yes we need to ensure that education prepares young people to yield to new experiences in a confident and intellectually curious manner. But the capacity to engage with change demands that they have an intellectual foundation from which they can set out in their quest to discover the future. That foundation is the legacy of human achievement, which is most effectively communicated through subject-based teaching. Standish's powerful critique of global education exposes the philistine motives that fuel its advocacy. Pointing the finger at global education, teachers, concerned citizens, and of course parents need to follow the example of that little boy who exclaimed that "the emperor has no clothes".

Frank Furedi
Professor of Sociology
University of Kent

Introduction

*Every child in the US needs 21st century knowledge
and skills to succeed as effective citizens, workers and
leaders in the 21st century . . . .There is a profound gap
between the knowledge and skills most students learn
in school and the knowledge and skills they need in typical
21st century communities and workplaces.*

PARTNERSHIP FOR 21ST CENTURY SKILLS[1]

This book is about the "gap" that is increasingly identified between what is being taught in schools and universities and what needs to be taught. The perception of this gap stems from a sense that the world has changed: that we are no longer living in homogenous communities bounded by national borders, but rather that we inhabit a global society that has placed new demands upon individuals. Schools that were built as institutions of national culture to nurture national citizens therefore need to be refashioned to teach global education and prepare global citizens. Similar arguments have been put forth in relation to colleges and universities.

Professor of Political Science Edward Kolodziej suggests that the "fundamental problems of deep and universal concern to humans everywhere can be resolved or managed only if they are addressed – *simultaneously and synchronously* – at local, national, regional, *and* global level . . . ," and that "the scope of these global and globalizing problems evidences the emergence of a global society for the first time in the evolution of the species" [author's emphasis].[2] Kolodziej asserts that interdisciplinary and interprofessional programs of study are necessary because, "the current diffuse and decentralized organization of educational programs and disciplinary units across the academy at all levels is ill-suited – in some instances a serious impediment – to the study of globalization and to the discovery of ways to employ and deploy the forces unleashed by globalization for human good, or, conversely, to limit and frustrate the damage they do."[3] The transition from national to global education is not only presented as the logical next step for humankind (part of its evolution), but also a necessary one as we adapt because "globalization has become the universal force that is passively pulling all nations of the Earth towards a common destiny."[4] New global realities are highlighted including the global market place, multicultural communities, and postnational politics. This global world is characterized by change and uncertainty, brought about by social and economic forces beyond the control of the nation state, and so knowledge and skills very quickly become outdated. In this fluid environment, knowledge of the past, the subject-based academic curriculum, is presented as less important than the skills for acquiring knowledge and working with others. Therefore, we are told, students need a different kind of education.

The rationale for global learning is primarily economic and moral. As Western economies flounder and some in the East thrive, education has increasingly been seen as the solution. "If we do not prepare to succeed in a highly competitive, knowledge-based, technology-driven global economy, we can expect the long-term decline in the earning power of our workers to continue and accelerate until we join the ranks of the second-rate powers," suggests the New Commission on the Skills of the American Workforce.[5] The New Commission adds that to avoid that outcome, "our whole population needs to be much better educated and very differently educated."[6] What it has in mind are qualities of "creativity and innovation, facility with the use of ideas and abstractions, the self-discipline and organization needed to manage one's work and drive it through to a successful conclusion, the ability to function well as a member of a team, and so on."[7] These are all qualities which one needs to succeed at work; indeed, skills needed for the global marketplace form a key part of global learning.

That education should be in service of the economy has reached the level of an almost unquestionable orthodoxy in the discussion of contemporary education. Wolfgang Sachs warns that the age of globalization education implicitly translates as "preparation for participation in the global economy."[8] Not surprisingly, corporations, as well as government, have been the main players advocating for teaching global skills for the global market.

The moral case for global education is different from the instrumental argument discussed above, but is similarly tied to theories of globalization. One definition suggests that global learning fosters "critical and creative thinking, self-awareness and open-mindedness towards difference, understanding of global issues and power relationships, and optimism and action for a better world."[9] Advocates for "global citizenship" seek to nurture children who are not tied to one culture or the nation state, but who work across boundaries to make connections with people from other cultures and world regions. Thus, it is suggested that the curriculum needs to reflect cosmopolitan values such as respect for diversity and tolerance, rather than national differences and cultural exceptionalism. The moral case for global education has been put forth by nonprofit organizations (especially those involved in environmental and development work), academics, government and intergovernmental bodies (especially UNESCO), and a minority of teachers.

The movement for global learning or education—sometimes termed "international education"—thus "solves a variety of problems, serves an array of masters, and expresses diverse and sometimes conflicting values," suggests Professor of Education Walter Parker.[10] Parker notes that global education is characterized by a lack of coherence, and a lack of precise terminology. This of course makes it difficult to study. However, this book seeks to clarify the discussion by analyzing the two strands identified above: the economic and moral cases for global education. What they both hold in common is a rejection of the national framework and the view of education as induction into academic knowledge and culture.

David Hicks observes that global education is both a field of study and also an umbrella term under which different educational initiatives and aims reside. Hicks recalls that global education emerged as a field of study in the late 1960s and 70s, incorporating the themes of interdependence, development, environment, racism, peace, and the future.[11] Since the mid-1990s, global education has been used in a more inclusive sense, encompassing international education, sustainable development education, global citizenship education, twenty-first-century skills, development education, human rights education, and other such "big" concepts. It is this more general, or global, use of the term with which this study is concerned. This more current usage of the term "global education" is allied to theories of globalization and the idea that we have entered a new Global Age.

The aim of this study is to explain the meaning of "global" in the context of education. We find that "global" is, today, decreasingly used as a geographical, political, or even cultural reference. Rather, it is used in a holistic sense, to mean breaking down boundaries. These are not necessarily geographical boundaries, but rather boundaries erected in the modern era: boundaries that define cultures, nations, subject-knowledge, the boundary between humanity and nature, and the boundary between education and social reform. In other words, "global" describes the global condition of humanity, as perceived in the eyes of its beholders.

This study takes a different approach from other texts about globalization and education. Rather than explaining global education as a response to "globalizing forces", it shows that the global turn is in fact a conscious choice by its advocates. Making education global has been used as a means to open up the term *education* to extrinsic moral reasoning. Put simply, when something is global it can include almost anything: training for the global market, global citizenship, taking action to resolve global issues, integrating multicultural communities, or self-awareness. By a similar token, the erosion of the line between education and social change is primarily a consequence of declining faith in the value of academic knowledge. As more people have come to question the value that academic subject-knowledge has to children, so they have filled schooling with alternative social concerns. Ralph Fevre describes this process as *demoralization*: the hollowing out of a social institution's moral purpose and replacing it with a rationale derived from a different social activity.[12]

Taking a critical approach to the global turn in education is not to assume that schools as institutions of national education were bastions of unencumbered liberal education (although very occasionally they were). Schools have rarely been free from instrumental social agendas.[13] However, although national education was created in the service of nation states, it also encompassed a rationale for education. For example, a 1914 US Bureau of Education report asserted that, "the primary objective in educating the people is to make good, intelligent, loyal, and prosperous citizen-sovereigns."[14] To become a citizen-sovereign in a liberal democracy necessitated the acquisition of at least a basic level of knowledge and skills, such that individuals could take responsibility for themselves and contribute to the economy, the political life of the nation, and reproduce society through the raising of offspring. This is not to be blind to the elitism and class structure of nation states, the instrumental purpose of educating loyal citizens, nor the fact that most children in state schools received a mediocre education, but simply to recognize that the socializing role of national schooling included the cultural affirmation of education through the acquisition of subject-knowledge. National schools were able to educate some children because education was grounded in a particular culture with collective identity and aspirations. This does not imply that schools should continue to teach the same knowledge and cultural traditions for the sake of preserving the past, as some on the Right would have it. Both knowledge and culture are dynamic and therefore should reflect new findings and cultural change. Schools should also teach children about other cultures so that they can reflect upon their own.

Nevertheless, education is moral when informed by the belief system of the community it serves. What is different about global education is that it inadvertently removes education from communities and specialists, the very people who are responsible for its moral content, and turns it into something else. Rather than passing on society's knowledge and morality, global educators and policy makers intend to use the curriculum to change the values of society or because it is the only way they know how to address economic stagnation. This book argues that in so doing, advocates of global education may have created a new rationale for schooling, but it is a rationale that has a degraded interpretation of education, which ultimately inhibits teaching children about the world. By expanding the meaning of education society is losing sight of what education is for.

This study focuses on two countries in which global education has been on the rise: the United States and England. As developed Western countries, they both exhibit confusion about the nature and purpose of education and have subsequently sought to import alternative rationales into schools; however, they have done so in quite different ways. The book focuses on primary and secondary education (grades kindergarten through 12), as both have been on the receiving end of global education initiatives. In places, references are also made to higher education, in recognition of similar discussions taking place about the need for global learning in its institutions. The focus on primary and secondary levels of education is simply a means to narrow the field of study. The methods used for this research include the following: content analysis of teaching materials, policy documents, guidelines, and other international/global education documents; interviews with teachers and other educators engaged with international or global education; interviews with individuals working for nonprofit organizations; observations of classroom lessons; and interviews with department heads/principals at schools that have embraced either a global or an international approach. Observations, samples of documentation, and teaching materials from the US and England are included throughout the text in order to illustrate the meaning and practice of global/international education.

Chapter 1 explores the origins and history of international education and global education in the United States and England. In particular, we show how international schools are very different in character from global education, in that they serve a particular community, and also distinguish between established centers of international education and more recent initiatives that have different aims for education. Chapter 2 details the rise of global learning over the past two decades, noting key differences between initiatives in England and the US. In Chapter 3, we learn that global knowledge opens up knowledge beyond expert-led subject knowledge, to promote the voices of minorities and children. This helps to make sense of the growing popularity of teaching about global issues and the future, rather than learning about knowledge of the past and present. Chapter 4 is about global skills. This includes skills for the global market and skills for global citizenship (personal, social, emotional, and learning skills). Global ethics are discussed in Chapter 5, although it is clear that these ethics often underpin the skills and knowledge discussed in the previous chapters. Global ethics include diversity, tolerance, empathy, social justice, environmental justice, peace, participation, interdependence, and human rights. We argue that the self-referential character of global ethics often inhibits a discussion of the social basis upon which education can proceed: a theme that we return to in Chapter 6. Here, we explore the boundaries that are necessary for education to be successful.

Notes

1 Partnership for 21st Century Skills (2009) "Mission". Accessed: http://www.p21.org/index.php?option=com_content&task= view&id=88&Itemid=110

2 Kolodziej (2005) p. 5.

3 Ibid. p. 6.

4 Wiggan and Hutchinson (2009) p. ix.

5 National Center on Education and the Economy (2007) p. 46.

6 Ibid. p. 46.

7 Ibid. p. xxv.

8 Sachs cited in Wiggan and Hutchinson (2009) p. 2.

9 Development Education Association (2011) About Global Learning. Accessed: http://www.think-global.org.uk/page.asp?p=3857

10 Parker (2009) p. 196.

11 Hicks (2007a) p. 5.

12 Fevre (2000).

13 Marsden (1989).

14 Cited in Nolan (1998) p. 139.

1

The origins of international and global education

International education has been around for some time. It has taken many different forms and been taught for a variety of ideological, academic, and pragmatic reasons. Scholars have long known that education can be a path to enlightenment, lifting individuals beyond the bounds of their limited experiences and resulting in diminished personal prejudice. Five hundred years ago, Desiderius Erasmus (1466–1536), a Roman Catholic Priest, wrote about the transformative potential of education to lessen a person's ties to a state or place. Educated by the Brethren of the Common Life in the Netherlands and at the University of Paris, Erasmus's concerns were in response to conflict between Protestants and Catholics in Europe. In the *Education of the Christian Prince,* Erasmus contended that the prince should study the liberal arts, theology, and literature in order to cultivate his ethical sensibilities and knowledge of human affairs.[1]

In modern times, most early movements for public schooling in America and Europe were unapologetically nationalistic in character. In the eighteenth and nineteenth centuries, ruling elites were concerned that the masses would develop their own ideas, become unruly, and undermine the capitalist system.[2] The upper classes wanted to ensure that the working classes were socially integrated, ready for work, and supportive of the nation. Thus, British schools promoted the benefits and wonders of the British Empire, while American schools were preoccupied with the maintenance of the Republic and integrating the flow of immigrants into American society. In the 1910s and 20s, the curriculum in the US schools sought to "Americanize" new arrivals through education and new rituals such as the Pledge of Allegiance.

However, not everyone was in favor of schooling children in national identity, especially during a time in which nationalism was strong. After both world wars there were calls for international or peace education, with the aim of increasing the understanding between youth in different nations. Similarly, cultural studies, which emphasized different cultural backgrounds rather than a homogenous Anglo-American culture, was first taught in the 1920s. Since this time, international education has taken a number of different forms, global education being one of them.

This chapter will describe the divergent approaches to education that have taken place at different times under the headings of international education, global education, world studies, or global studies. We will begin with a brief history of international schools so that we can distinguish between these and the disparate forms of international and global education that grew out of the cultural conditions of the 1960s and 70s.

International schools

An oft cited starting date for international education is 1924, the year in which the International School of Geneva was opened for children of parents working at the newly founded League of Nations. This was the first of several new international schools established in the 1920s and 1930s. But international schooling predates the 1920s; Brickman cites thirty formal plans for international education between 1814 and 1914, including Spring Grove School in west London (1866), the International School of Peace in Boston (1910), and international schools at Chatou near Paris and Bad Godesberg near Bonn.[3] These schools were supported by philanthropists, intellectuals such as Thomas Huxley and John Tyndall, and organizations promoting peace and international collaboration, including the International Bureau of New Schools in Geneva (1899), the American School Peace League (1908) in

Boston, and Carnegie Endowment for International Peace (1910). Yet it was the scale of the destructiveness of the Great War, the millions of deaths and hundreds of destroyed towns and cities, which amplified the calls for international cooperation and the curtailment of nationalism.

To this end, the Institute of International Education was established in New York City in 1919. A few years later, the National Education Association (NEA) held a world conference on education in San Francisco for the promotion of "goodwill and mutual understanding" in schools.[4] The popularity of international education grew over the decade. A 1932 address by Augustus Thomas, the Secretary General of the World Federation of Education Associations, to the NEA in Atlantic City called for a world-wide plan of education for understanding and cooperation among nations, a curriculum with an international framework, and teachers trained with an international perspective.[5] Developments were similarly afoot in Europe, with Geneva proving to be a hub for the promotion of international education. A year after the international school was opened the International Bureau of Education was founded in Geneva by the Institute JJ Rousseau. The Council for Education in World Citizenship, founded in 1939, took over the educational work of the League of Nations and was later instrumental in the creation of the United Nations Educational, Scientific, and Cultural Organization (UNESCO). Although small in number, international schools could now be found in England, Holland, Switzerland, Germany, Denmark, France, and the United States. International education was not restricted to Western nations; Indian writer Rabindranath Tagore established an international school and world university near Calcutta in 1918, and the Yokohama International School in Japan was opened for children of foreigners in 1924.

After the Second World War, the theme of international education was taken up by the United Nations. Like the League of Nations in Geneva, a United Nations International School was established in New York City (1947) to serve the children of United Nations employees. UNESCO was specifically charged with the task of building international education: established in 1945, UNESCO's stated aim is to "build peace in the minds of men and women" because it is in people's heads that wars are started.[6] Kenan Malik notes that the formation of UNESCO was a conscious decision by the leaders of the postwar alliance, taken in order to move away from the racist ideas associated with the biological view of humanity. UNESCO Man was a cultural being, not a biological one. However, Malik finds that instead of promoting a universal cultural being, UNESCO's battle against barbarism replaced racial divisions with cultural pluralism. "Just as race once determined every aspect of human behavior, so now culture did the same."[7] In UNESCOs view, international education was concerned with promoting values of respect for different cultures: promoting, rather than transcending, difference.

One of UNESCO's early ventures was the Conference of Principles of International Schools in Paris in 1949, attended by representatives of fifteen interested schools from across Europe and the US. Over subsequent decades, UNESCO has been instrumental in the promotion, direction, and coordination of international education, especially in Europe and North America. This it did through organizing conferences, writing key documents on international education, and supporting initiatives at the national level.

It is important not to treat all international schools or international education initiatives as the same. Today, there are over one thousand international schools worldwide, which vary in terms of how they define their international standing. Schools describe themselves as international for a number of reasons, such as "the nature of the student population and of the curriculum offered, marketing and competition with other schools in the area, and the school's overall ethos or mission."[8]

There are at least three rationales for the existence of international schools: pragmatic, economic, and ideological. International schools often open in a country to serve the needs of employees who have relocated to that country, frequently on a temporary basis, and who wish their children to receive a similar curriculum and be taught in the same language as that provided by schools back home. Such schools provide "globally mobile expatriates with a cultural bubble by isolating their children's educational environment from exposure to local culture."[9] Such schools frequently teach in English and may serve children from a variety of countries. Mary Hayden notes that teaching in English is often the main attraction for parents who view English as an international language that will help their children in the global job market, and learning a second language is often viewed as an additional marketable skill.

Hayden also remarks that parents value internationally recognized qualifications, such as the International Baccalaureate and International GCSEs (General Certificate in Secondary Education). The International Baccalaureate Organization (IBO) was founded in Geneva in 1968 to provide the transnationally mobile with a qualification recognized by colleges, universities, and employers across the world. Its aim was to facilitate the "international mobility of students preparing for university by providing schools with a curriculum and diploma qualification recognized by universities around the world."[10] As a part of the Economic and Social Council of the United Nations, it also reflects the values and aims of the United Nations. Hence, international schools often arise for pragmatic and economic reasons in response to the wishes of transnationally mobile parents; and, as the number of transnational corporations has grown over the past couple of decades, the demand for international schools has increased.

Some international schools also promote the cause of international-mindedness, as noted above. Historically, this meant promoting solidarity across borders and a view that social, economic, and political progress could be achieved through international cooperation rather than competition between nations. For instance, Washington International School, located in Washington DC, serves parents who have come to the US capital from numerous different countries, as well as American parents who wish their children to receive an internationally orientated education. This is achieved through a broad subject-based curriculum, learning more than one language, an International Baccalaureate qualification, and learning about different cultural traditions. Such international schools focus upon education in a common body of knowledge, much like public schools, but with an emphasis upon cultural variation rather than national values.

However, Hayden notes that there is sometimes a disparity between the educational values of parents and the values of international educators. She suggests that many parents value international schools for providing instruction in English and subject-based qualifications that have a good standing in the Western world. In contrast, those working in the field of international education are more likely to emphasize ideological aims. Today, these aims are likely to coincide with those of global education, which seeks to move away from a curriculum that is Western-centric in terms of subject content and culture.

Strands of international/ global education

There are many approaches that fall under the umbrella of "international" or "global" education. Summarized below, some approaches are knowledge-based, while others are skills- or values-based. For a more detailed background to the teaching of international education, see *American Education in a Global Society: Internationalizing Teacher Education* by Gerald Gutek.[11]

Intercultural education

Intercultural education aims to help children overcome limited cultural experiences. This has been approached in different ways at different times and includes international travel and learning foreign languages. If education involves expanding the mind and one's experiences, stepping outside of one's culture and language is an essential part of that process. Only by gaining insight into the language and culture of people in other countries can one learn to see past the limitations and cultural biases of one's homeland, to bridge cultural divides and comprehend our common humanity. This aim has been integral to many versions of international education, as well as liberal education and comprehensive education (as in England). Learning about foreign cultures and languages can take place in a formal class setting, through writing letters, Internet communication with foreign students, and guest speakers, but often pupils are encouraged to spend time in another country so that they gain a wider cultural experience. This may happen through a period of study abroad or a student exchange program.

In Europe, schools have an established tradition of foreign languages as part of the curriculum. While classical education included the study of Greek and Latin, most schools later replaced these with learning another European language. The teaching of English in continental Europe has perhaps been most successful, aided by its significance as an international language. In the US, European languages have also been dominant, with Spanish especially being taught from primary level. Nevertheless, intercultural education has historically focused on the diversity of culture within America; as a nation of immigrants, it is no surprise that intercultural education has flourished here. One pioneer of intercultural teaching was Rachel DuBois, who worked at a New Jersey High School in the 1920s, later taking a seat on the Service Bureau for Intercultural Education. DuBois taught about discrimination and inequality and focused on the lives and stories of the pupils in her classes. Two decades later, in 1945, the National Council for the Social Studies published *Democratic Human Relations: Promising Practices in Intergroup and Intercultural Education in the Social Studies*.[12] Edited by Hilda Taba and William van Til, the bulletin was a bestseller in the education profession.

In the late 1960s and 70s, intercultural education, now in the form of multicultural education, became a central philosophy in American schools. This development reflected the demands of the civil rights movement for the equal inclusion of minorities in American society. Schools were asked to play a central role in integrating children from different cultural backgrounds into a more inclusive definition of America. The multicultural approach emphasized respect and appreciation for cultural differences within American society. Much like UNESCO Man, multiculturalism encouraged children to focus on, and respect, cultural difference rather than search for a common humanity. In the 1980s and 90s, multiculturalism became an increasingly dominant feature of European societies and schooling, reflecting the decline of distinctive national cultures and confident nationalistic identities.

The rise of the multicultural orthodoxy has caused a dramatic change in the content of intercultural education, which now has less to do with educating children about different cultural settings and more to do with the promotion of cultural identity. It is notable, for example, that despite the rhetoric of globalization and the emphasis placed upon intercultural-communication, there are fewer pupils studying foreign languages today in both the US and England. As is explored in Chapter 4, the emphasis upon cultural interaction is not being matched by a sustained commitment to teaching world languages and culture to children.

Peace studies

Many advocates of international education have been motivated by a desire to bring peace between nations. Peace studies evolved as an academic field through research centers and graduate schools in North America and Europe following the Second World War and has been defined as "the systematic interdisciplinary study of the causes of war and the conditions of peace."[13] The field attracted further interest in the 1970s alongside the civil rights movement and the Vietnam War. By the 1980s it had expanded into undergraduate curricula and schools, receiving backing from private sources and the state. For instance, Congress established the US Institute for Peace in 1984.

Peace studies is an interdisciplinary subject, the objective of which is to influence policy in a given direction: toward conflict resolution by mediation rather than by war. By its very nature, it is concerned with international or global concerns, but seeks to understand these through a world systems approach. Some peace studies advocates think it necessary to understand the interplay between the interests of nation states and to find peaceful ways to resolve conflicts of interest. Others see the nation state and sovereignty as "a major obstacle to the development of global institutions needed for peacekeeping and peacemaking."[14] A further distinction is between those who see peace as the absence of war (negative peace) and those who want to resolve the causes of war, by bringing about economic and social justice (positive peace).

The causes of conflict are sometimes portrayed as originating in the minds of individuals: as one of the founders of peace education, Betty Reardon, explains, "the fundamental causes of violence, war and oppression lie in the way we think."[15] With this approach, students are encouraged to view conflict along a continuum, from the psychology of the individual to the group to global conflict, and education is seen as a direct vehicle for building a more peaceful world, by changing the way students think.

Development education

Development education and development studies grew in the aftermath of the Second World War, during the era of decolonization. Development education provided one way for Western nations to continue a relationship with former colonies, and also created space for nonprofit organizations to operate in underdeveloped countries. It thus became the prerogative of intergovernmental organizations, such as UNESCO, and international nonprofits alike.

In schools, lessons included examples of large-scale projects such as the construction of dams, as well as smaller projects to provide clean water, materials for schools, and food aid. In this way, development education became a way of promoting the West's postcolonial role as a positive one, in contrast to its more problematic imperial past.

Over recent decades nonprofit organizations have become a significant source of teaching materials for schools, as well as offering some teacher training. In the UK, there are over forty development education centers that coordinate the educational work of nonprofits. In the US, the role of nonprofits is less formalized, but no less influential. Nonprofit organizations view education as an important means of communicating their message, and development studies has opened up a space through which this message is readily embraced.

Human rights education

During the post-World War II period, human rights became codified by the United Nations in the Universal Declaration of Human Rights, the United Nations Charter, and International Covenants on Economic, Social and Cultural Rights, and Political and Civil Rights. Signed on December 10, 1948, at the General Assembly, the Universal Declaration was the first attempt to create an international document concerning people's rights. It drew ideas from the Magna Carta, the French Declaration of the Rights of Man, the American Declaration of Independence, and the US Bill of Rights. The Universal Declaration contains political rights such as the right to a fair trial, freedom of speech, religion and assembly, and the presumption of innocence; and economic, social and cultural rights including the right to an equal pay for equal work, the right to social security, to work and protection against unemployment, and the right to education.

Human rights education has grown alongside international and global education, and many see them as inseparable. Until recent years, the most significant document on international education was the 1974 UNESCO publication *Recommendations Concerning Education for International Understanding, Co-operation and Peace and Education Relating to Human Rights and Fundamental*

Freedoms. The document asserted that international understanding, cooperation, and peace "cannot be achieved without successful efforts to promote the protection of human rights."[16] Although the report was not a mandate for action, human rights has become integrated into school curricula in both the US and England. In general, the promotion of human rights education and the production of teaching resources about human rights has fallen to many institutions including universities, civil rights organizations, voluntary and religious groups, private foundations, and other nonprofit organizations, including Amnesty International, The Fund for Peace, and the Human Rights Education Association.

Human rights education involves learning about human rights and instances where they are/are not upheld, and also developing attitudes and values conducive to support for human rights. Lessons frequently explore examples of instances in which people's human rights are threatened: natural disasters, persecution, slavery, refugees, and discrimination. Many of these problems are found in developing countries, which are the main focus of human rights education.

Foreign policy and area/regional studies

International education is viewed by some as a means to further national self-interest. This has especially been the case when nations have engaged themselves in foreign conquest or conflict. Britain is the archetypal example here: from the time that public schooling became a national priority in the late nineteenth century, education in British schools was concerned with teaching children about the Empire and instilling a sense of pride in the nation's colonial possessions. The place of geography in the school curriculum was connected to its suitability to the study of colonies and other distant lands—Halford Mackinder, the pioneer of political geography, promoted the subject because it could be used to teach pupils to visualize the world, "think imperially" and learn to see the world as a "theatre for British activity."[17] In parallel with the decline of Empire, geography in England suffered something of an identity crisis. The content of geography in textbooks became less international and more focused on the UK as the twentieth century progressed.[18] Conversely, in the American curriculum, the prominence of knowledge about the rest of the world increased as the United States rose to a position of global leadership.[19]

Here, the different histories of the US and Great Britain are in evidence. Gutek recalls that for much of its existence the American nation espoused a perspective of isolationism, Manifest Destiny, and self-righteousness.[20] This ideal reflected the desire of European settlers to break from religious intolerance and the imperial designs of their nations of origin. The common school movement communicated this sentiment through local organization and a policy of assimilation. Although the US fought the Spanish-American War of 1898 and played a significant role in the Great War, Gutek notes that isolationism persisted until World War II. Symptomatic of this perspective was the refusal of the Senate to ratify the League of Nations Agreement that Woodrow Wilson obtained at Versailles in 1918. Yet, at the end of the Second World War, America assumed its place as the new global hegemon, and its policy of isolationism was confined to the past. American attitudes were to change and so would its inward-looking curriculum. A turning point in American education was 1957, the launching of the Soviet satellite Sputnik. Fear of falling behind in the Cold War prompted the 1958 National Defense Education Act, which, through its Title VI Program, funded foreign language and area studies centers at universities throughout the nation. Today, there are 125 National Resource Centers for Foreign Language, Area, and International Studies supported through the Department of Education.

From the 1950s, new courses in world geography and world history were introduced in schools to teach pupils not only about the rest of the world, but also how American interests were best served with respect to different countries. Jones and Murphy's *Geography and World Affairs*[21] is one example of a widely used textbook that took a geopolitical approach; world history courses were similarly focused on Cold War conflict.

Global education/world studies

In contrast to international education, global education (or world studies as it was originally called in England) seeks to surpass the nation state and national interest, encouraging children to see themselves as global citizens who together can address global issues. Hence, their aims are in sympathy with peace education, development education, and human rights education. According to Kenneth Tye, global education involves:

> [L]earning about problems and issues that cut across national boundaries, and about the interconnectedness of systems – ecological, cultural, economic, political, and technological. Global education involves perspective taking – seeing things through the eyes and minds of others – and it means the realization that while individuals and groups may view life differently, they also have common needs and wants.[22]

Thus, global education and world studies run counter to the idea that education is a means of inducting children into knowledge and culture through a subject-based curriculum. Instead, global education means studying real-world problems, engaging with them, and learning to see issues from the perspective of others. According to Jan Tucker, global education emerged out of a report by the Foreign Policy Association, titled "An Examination of the Objectives and Priorities in International Education in US Secondary and Elementary Schools."[23] The report prompted a special issue of the journal *Social Education* titled "International Education for the Twenty-first Century", edited by Lee Anderson and James Becker. This publication took a global approach because it "rejected the idea of international education as a study of a collection of nations," writes Tye.[24]

Global education and world studies are frequently concerned with the values and attitudes of pupils. Through studying global issues it is hoped that children will surpass their attachment to nation states and work cooperatively to help those in need. An experiential and interdisciplinary approach to the study of problems is often preferred over subject mastery. Pupils explore a range of international issues including environmental problems, malnutrition, health problems, natural disasters, and other challenges of development. Environmental education and, later, education for sustainable development, became a key part of global education and world studies. The first wave of global and world studies coincided with the counter-cultural movement of the 1960s and 1970s, and is explored in greater detail below. The second wave began in the 1990s and resulted in more profound change to American and English schooling. The second wave is discussed in Chapter 2.

Environmental education/sustainable development education

Environmental education became a popular topic in American schools during the 1970s, alongside the growth of the environmental movement. It was introduced to schools in the form of several projects backed by environmental nonprofits, with backing of the US Office of Education and the 1970 Environmental Education Act. These included Project Learning Tree, Project Wild, Project WET (Water Education for Teachers), and Project GREEN (Global Rivers Environmental Education Network). The aim of environmental education was to produce a "citizenry that is knowledgeable concerning the biophysical environment and its associated problems, aware of how to help solve these problems, and motivated to work towards their solution," suggested William Stapp.[25] Since the 1970s, environmental education has remained an important part of the curriculum in American schools, but is often subsumed across subjects. A second Environmental Act in 1990 authorized a wider network of organizations, grants, and awards related to environmental education, including an Office of Environmental Education as part of the Environmental Protection Agency. Today, it is focused on different issues such as climate change and resource consumption, and is often discussed in terms of personal responsibility.[26] Environmental education also crossed the Atlantic to England, being incorporated into Schools' Council Projects and World Studies in the 1970s and 80s. Again, the approach taken in schools often depended upon the interests and work of particular teachers. However, in the 1980s and 90s, sustainable development became the dominant framework for environmental ideas in Europe. The idea of sustainable development has a history dating back to the Tbilisi Declaration (1977), the World Commission on Environment and Development (1987), and the Earth Summit in Rio de Janeiro (1992). By the late 1990s, sustainable development was identified as an aim of education in the English national curriculum.

Sustainable development is usually defined as "development that meets the needs of the present generation without compromising the ability of future generations to meet their own needs."[27] As such, it is commonsensical. Nevertheless, it also implies much more than this, including an emphasis on the need to develop harmony with the natural world and skepticism toward large-scale development projects and industrialization. Commitment to sustainable development is a key part of global education. While environmental education in the 1970s was grass-roots-led, sustainable development from the 1990s has been promoted from the top down, by government and intergovernmental organizations. The United Nations has been a keen advocate, proclaiming 2005–14 to be the "UN Decade of Education for Sustainable Development." Sustainable development has been less prominent in the American curriculum, although in recent years some states have included the language of sustainability in their standards.

Education for a global market

From the 1980s onward, the business community and political leaders looked to schools as a means to provide children with a different set of skills and attitudes considered appropriate to a more flexible and internationally orientated economy. Multinational employers were looking for graduates who were comfortable doing business with companies based overseas and sensitive to foreign markets and cultures. Now some governors, mayors, policy makers, and politicians were joining the ranks of those advocating for international and global education in schools. For instance, an influential report published by the American National Governors Association – *America in Transition: The International Frontier* (1989)—asserted that "international education must be an integral part of the education of every student."[28] The report outlined the need for more young people conversant in foreign languages, for teachers to know more about international issues, and for the business community to support international education so that they have access to information about export markets, trade regulations, and overseas cultures.

This global market rationale for international and global education came later than the other strands of international education, but it has become a key part of global education in twenty-first century schools. It has also strengthened the idea that education should be in service of the economy. Global skills for the global market are considered in Chapter 4.

Defining the terms

At this stage it should be evident to readers that clarity of terminology is not a feature of the discussion of global education. Furthermore, it is not uncommon for people to use some of these terms interchangeably, switching between international education, global education, global learning, world studies, and also making links to citizenship education. In our view, this lack of precision in terminology is indicative of an absence of consensus among its various advocates, and society more broadly, about the purpose and content of education. Indeed, it is because of the broader crisis of educational purpose today that concepts of international and global education have grown in popularity.

What should be clear from the brief summary above is that very different ideas have been expressed in the name of international or global education. In the 1960s and 70s, two strands of global thinking emerged: those who use global ideas with a view to advancing their political and economic power beyond national borders, and those who see the global as a postnational, postmodern human condition. The former portrays the global as an extension of the national. For Western nations, the global Cold War became a defense of their political and economic system, their way of life. As the national consensus ebbed, the global contest became increasingly important for the "management of domestic affairs" by politicians[29]; citizens might disagree on many things, but at least they could be rallied against the Red Menace. When the sun finally set on the Cold War, the shallowness of this negative justification of national values was exposed. On the other side, those on the radical Left, the postnationalists, were rejecting modernist assumptions about history, progress, nature, and society. What both sides had in common was the extent to which they looked to education to further their cause.

Global thinking

Amid the social upheaval and political turmoil of the 1960s and 70s, many began to question authority based upon past traditions and perceive that society was moving into a new period. Key to this sentiment was a profound sense of detachment from the past. Global theorists focused their attention on new conditions, such as the increased cooperation and integration between nation states on an "unprecedented" scale. While the interwar years had witnessed a contraction of international trade, the post-World War II period was one in which trade deals between nations grew rapidly.[30] Other changes that are considered to have contributed to a growth of global thinking include: the possibility of nuclear war, which for the first time posed a potential threat to humanity as a whole, rather than just one nation state; and the first photographs of the whole Earth taken from space, which for the first time allowed humanity to view its entire planet from afar (Figure 1).

FIGURE 1   Apollo 8: Earthrise: the lunar horizon is 350 miles from the spacecraft, while the Earth is 240,000 miles distant (December 22nd, 1968).[31]

Lee Anderson, one of the founders of global education in the United States, argues that four conditions had given rise to the new global age: the unprecedented international character of world affairs; the increasingly globalized human condition; the globalization of the history, geography, economics, politics, and sociology of humanity; and the trend toward a world system.[32] By "globalized human condition" Anderson means that many trends in society were accelerating exponentially and could not be sustained. In his thesis on the global age, Anderson illustrates a number of "J" curves to demonstrate the exponential growth induced by humanity, including population, circulation of money, books published, life expectancy, speed of communication, atmospheric carbon dioxide, energy consumption, and fertilizer use. All of these, argues Anderson, had driven nation states to work together in ways that had not been thought of in previous times; hence, the condition of humanity has become *globalized*, as we are propelled together in time and space to such a degree that our world system becomes interdependent.

While global thinking held its attractions for Left-wing liberals, some national leaders also reacted to the eroding national consensus by turning to global agendas, such as environmental problems and human rights. Officials in the 1970s were warning of impending environmental catastrophe, a line of thought captured in the 1972 Club of Rome report *Limits to Growth*. U Thant, then Secretary General of the United Nations, warned that we had just ten years to save the planet through a "global partnership to curb the arms race, to improve the human environment, to diffuse the population explosion, and to supply the required momentum to development efforts."[33] Official backing for international education was provided at a UNESCO conference and its report *Recommendations Concerning Education for International Understanding, Co-operation and Peace and Education Relating to Human Rights and Fundamental Freedom*.[34] The conference highlighted the potential of the curriculum to promote "understanding, tolerance and friendship amongst all nations, racial and religious groups and further the activities of the United Nations for the maintenance of peace."[35] Support for international education and peace studies was by no means unanimous. Some American and British government advisers were suspicious of this approach and condemned it as unpatriotic, soft on communism, and academically weak.[36]

The first wave of global education

Alternatives to the national, subject-based curriculum grew rapidly on both sides of the Atlantic during and after the counter-cultural and civil rights movement of the 1960s and 70s. These included peace studies, environmental education, world studies, global studies, human rights education, development education, and multicultural education. The timing of this rise in alternative pedagogy was no accident: it took place during a period in which the ruling ideas of national elites were being challenged on several fronts by campaigns that were antiwar and antinuclear, but prominority rights and proenvironmentalism. Having led their people through two world wars, an economic depression, colonial oppression, and the experience of the Holocaust and the atomic bomb, Western leaders were struggling to articulate a positive defense of the modern world. New social movements provided an alternative political narrative, the starting point of which was a rejection of the national political framework and its intellectual and cultural traditions. Thus, the causes of new social movements were frequently not tied to the fate of nation states, rather their aims were directed at uniting oppressed minorities across national borders, saving the environment, or preventing war between nations.

Over time, many new social movements became professionalized as nongovernmental or not-for-profit organizations and integrated into mainstream society. By transitioning into officialdom, these organizations became less connected to their grass-roots origins and also less antiestablishment. Concerns for ecological matters, peace, aiding the Third World, human rights, and nuclear disarmament became the work of groups like Oxfam, Greenpeace, Save the Children, Amnesty International, the Campaign for Nuclear Disarmament, Peace Corps, and Médecins Sans Frontières (Doctors without Borders). These international causes drew support from religious groups, those concerned for social welfare, and often also from teachers. The seemingly bipartisan nature of these issues provided the opportunity for teachers to incorporate them into their curriculum, while the fragmented cultural mood of the times encouraged radical thinking to flourish. A network of nonprofits, with branches dedicated to the production of supplemental materials and training for teachers, grew to promote their causes through schools (including environmental, peace, human rights, and development groups).

Educating for a global perspective

Education, as a gateway between the past and the future, has often demonstrated sensitivity to the discussion of social stability and change. It is the job of teachers, and also parents, to prepare children for the world which they will inherit as adults. In many societies, adults have sought to prepare children for the future by educating them about the past and the present. This means passing on to the next-generation intellectual and cultural traditions. But what happens when the authority of societal knowledge and culture is called into question? Teachers need to have confidence in that which they are teaching children, otherwise they cannot do their job effectively.

As Simon Fisher explains in a world studies text, teachers are in a difficult position—"committed to helping young people equip themselves for a life which will largely be spent in the twenty-first century, yet having little clear idea of what conditions will be like and facing conflicting views on which attitudes and trends should be supported and which resisted."[37] But of course we never know precisely what the future will hold. When society retains a modicum of consensus about the principles upon which it is founded, combined with a vision of where it is heading, equipping children to play their part in a future society is not problematic. It is only when faced with uncertainty about themselves or a lack of confidence in their ability to handle the future that adults become unsure about what to teach. It is this vacuum that has created the space for advocates of global education to assert their alternative notions of education.

In 1968, four years after McLuhan coined the term "global village," one author laid out a new vision for schooling: "Preparing young people to live creatively and cooperatively instead of destructively in this village is a major responsibility of schools."[38] During the 1960s and 70s, the subject-based curriculum was criticized as a Western, white, and male-dominated view of the world, which was utilized to perpetuate social hierarchy and oppression, to the exclusion of other people's part in history and world affairs.[39] However, it was less clear what would take its place. For young people to be prepared for living in a global age, Anderson asserted that the content, methods, and social context of education needed to be revised. He suggested that the curriculum should move away from a perspective that was Euro-North American-centric, group-centric, state-centric, anthropocentric, past-centric, and spectator-centric toward one that was based on a *global perspective*. In this respect, global education is "as much a point of view or outlook as a program."[40] Intrinsic to a global perspective are:

1 An understanding of the earth and its inhabitants as parts of an interrelated network,

2 An awareness that there are some alternatives facing individual nations and the human species, and that choices made will shape our future world,

3 An ability to recognize that others may have different perceptions and may prefer different choices.[41]

In this view, having a global perspective is not simply about replacing one worldview with another. It also means not asserting that one way of viewing the world is better than another. It thus encapsulates an attitude of relativism, through which children are expected to construct their own knowledge and choose their own values rather than receive an education grounded in a particular culture and worldview.

In perceiving that moral and intellectual wisdom resides within the individual rather than society, global education is also a form of progressive education, which views education as the unfolding or development of the inner being,[42] and can be traced back to the nineteenth-century Romantic Movement and the work of individuals such as Jean-Jacques Rousseau. Advocates of progressive education view didactic instruction as an imposition on the inner-self, which is likely to curtail the pupil's creative spirit.

The influence of progressive education in the 1960s and 70s also helps to account for the centrality of environmental ideas to global education. This reveals that behind the cross-cultural and values-neutral veneer, there are strong assumptions about the human condition—as it is, and as it should be—that inform the teaching of global perspectives. These include being nonjudgmental toward other cultures and ideas, and a belief that environmental considerations should trump human activity.

The outlook underpinning a global perspective was made explicit in a landmark paper written by Robert Hanvey in 1976, titled "An Attainable Global Perspective." Hanvey outlined five dimensions for educators: perspectives consciousness (recognizing that others have different viewpoints), state of planet awareness (the dangers of exponential growth), cross-cultural awareness (recognizing diversity of ideas and practices), knowledge of global dynamics (interconnectivity), and awareness of human choices (there are alternative futures). In addition to acceptance of other ideas and cultural practices, Hanvey explained his underlying pessimism with respect to the growth of population and the consumption of resources:

Before very long the world system is going to break down. That doesn't mean total catastrophe but it does mean that the system will suffer some terrible shocks. The reason for the impending breakdown is that population, resource consumption, and pollution are growing exponentially. Since the world population is already large, since many nonrenewable resources are almost used up, since the environment's capacity to absorb pollutants is already strained, such growth cannot be considered benign. Exponential growth is treacherously rapid and will bring us to the earth's finite limits – and thus to a condition of stress – within a few generations.[43]

Gaining a global perspective is this respect means questioning the potential of humanity to continue to expand resources by finding new and better ways to use natural or synthetic materials. When globalists assert the interconnectivity of people and nature, they do so to encourage society to respect what they view as the limits of nature.

Some globalists subscribe to the Gaian theory, as depicted by James Lovelock in the 1970s. Gaia was the Greek goddess of the Earth; Lovelock asserted that Earth, as a holistic system, was *alive*. He also believed that organic and inorganic materials should not be viewed as separate, but part of an interconnected whole. In Gaian thought, humanity is an integral part of nature and hence should not be using up natural resources at unsustainable rates. Mary Midgley explains:

Earth is not a heap of inert resources but a self maintaining system which acts as a whole. It can therefore be injured, it is vulnerable, capable of health or sickness. And, since we are totally dependent on it, we are vulnerable too.[44]

Hanvey, Anderson, Lovelock, and others wanted children to think critically about the way the world was and to consider alternative futures. This involved questioning modernist assumptions about economic development and cultural progress, with an emphasis on shaping nature to meet human needs, and subscribing instead to an approach that saw people in harmony with nature and each other. The trajectory of nation states, in this view, was part of the problem of modernization, and the teaching of traditional subject knowledge represented the imposition of Western values, which globalists saw as part of the problem. This was the context in which problem solving and discovery learning became promoted as a desired alternative to education in national knowledge and culture. Hanvey and Anderson proposed that education be less about the transmission of abstractions and established knowledge, and more geared around an approach that castes pupils in active roles, engaged in concrete learning tied to the child's personal experiences. "The key to education is enquiry rather than knowledge itself," suggests Simon Fisher's handbook on world studies.[45]

A first wave of global education in the United States

With the first wave of global education, we can see the influence of those struggling to find a narrative to support American global hegemony running alongside the different agenda of postmodernists and progressive educators. In 1966, an International Education Act was passed, the main aim of which was to add international content to the curriculum. This Act was in keeping with America's growing international role and the perceived need for citizens to be more aware of international issues and foreign policy. It was during this period that National Resource Centers for Foreign Language, Area, and International Studies were established, such as the Institute for Latin American Studies at the University of Texas, Austin. The Act was followed by a Task Force on Global Education. Launched by Commissioner Earnest L. Boyer, its remit was to examine the need for a global perspective in American schools. The task force reported that "global education contributes to a fundamental competence in a world context, to educational excellence, and to the nation's vital interests."[46] It endorsed a new grant program to assist with the expansion of teaching about global perspectives and to incorporate global education into existing US Department of Education programs.

Meanwhile, courses in global studies were becoming popular in some schools, frequently through partnerships with universities or independent research centers. One often-cited project is the Columbus in the World program. A product of the Mershon Center and the College of Education at Ohio State University, this initially involved graduate students collating an inventory of community connections to other states and nations. This included banking, medicine, religion, labor, real estate, resources, education, agriculture, sports, media, and business. The inventory was then used to produce teaching materials in schools, such as the textbook *Windows on Our World*, which aimed to help citizens to "make more informed judgments about the ways in which their own community and jobs are interdependent with the world."[47] While such an inventory would certainly enlighten community members and pupils as to the many ways in which their lives were connected beyond their immediate territory, the project also sought to challenge the "traditional bifurcation of domestic and foreign policy" as "in essence nonsense."[48]

In California, the Center for Human Interdependence was also actively promoting global education in schools in the 1970s. It assisted some fifteen schools in adopting the global approach through units called "Global Awareness through Family History," "Discovering the World in Our Backyard," and "How Interdependent Are We?" Another example comes from Dade County, Miami, where two high schools, North Miami Beach and Miami South Ridge, implemented programs based on Hanvey's global perspectives model. These schools were also supported by a higher education partnership: the Global Awareness Program at Florida International University. Other early US initiatives for global education included, the University of Minnesota's social studies curriculum center; the model United Nations Program; and UN teaching units such as "Teaching About Global Interdependence in a Peaceful World." On the West Coast, examples include the Bay Area China Project and Diablo Valley Education Project, produced in association with the Rosenberg Foundation.

The success of such initiatives often depended upon the enthusiasm of the teachers. Some were maintained, while others tailored off. One of the main differences between this early movement and global education today is that it was a minority movement that by no means pervaded mainstream curricula. "Attempts to introduce global education into curricula have met with limited success," acknowledged Klein and Tye in 1979.[49]

More widespread change to the American curriculum was to come in the 1980s, with the resurgence of Right-wing rhetoric, the Cold War, and a backlash against the "permissiveness" of previous decades. Alternative and radical agendas were pushed to the margins. A number of states lined up behind an internationally orientated curriculum. New Jersey, California, Massachusetts, Florida, New York, Missouri, Illinois, and Washington all published guidelines for global or international education. For example, *Education for a Global Perspective: A Plan for New York State* was released by New York State Department of Education in 1983; while in Illinois, the focus was on the social studies curriculum: *Increasing International and Intercultural Comparisons through Social Studies* (1988). This change was picked up by education publishers who provided the necessary textbooks and more schools moved to teach courses in world studies, global studies, world history, and world geography. New York, for example, required pupils to take two years of global studies over grades nine and ten (age: 14–16), and Oregon mandated that all high school graduates take a course in global studies. Pupils in these states were still taught American history, but the emphasis upon America's uniqueness and the need to build loyalty to the nation were replaced by an objective to develop an "understanding of the interrelationships between peoples, countries and continents."[50] In the words of the late Samuel Huntington, American leaders had begun the process of "merging America with the world."[51]

A first wave of global education in England

In England, early projects for global or alternative curricula received some backing from both governmental and nongovernmental sources. The World Studies Project (1973–80) was launched by the One World Trust with financial support from Department of

Education and Science, the Leverhulme Trust, and the Ministry for Overseas Development. The project's aim was "to encourage modification of syllabuses at secondary school level to reflect a world perspective rather than national attitudes."[52] In England, world studies was heavily influenced by an array of voluntary organizations, associations, and agencies. In 1979, a Department for Education and Sciences catalogue listed 115 such groups.[53] The developing world has been a primary concern for many groups; in 1966, the Voluntary Committee on Overseas Aid and Development was created to coordinate the educational activities of organizations like Oxfam and Christian Aid, but was later replaced by the Centre for World Development Education.

This project was followed in the 1980s by World Studies 8–13, produced by the Schools' Council and the Joseph Rowntree Trust. This program offered a multicultural approach to education and aimed to develop international understanding.[54] Lessons in world studies were designed to help pupils cope with global issues, to clarify their own values, study cultures different from their own, and consider how the world could be different. Fisher recalls that world studies necessitated reflecting at different levels: "How would we like things to be in the world as a whole, in our country, locally, for me?"[55] For instance, in a lesson titled "Which Way to World Peace?," pupils were asked to "imagine that the world's people have had enough of war" and so will hold an election to "choose the people best able to ensure that peace and justice will come about."[56] This was a values clarification exercise in which pupils had to decide candidates through a discussion of the personal qualities and positions of each candidate. The objective was to help pupils "develop and clarify their images of peace and justice." Other examples of world studies lessons include identifying where population and wealth were concentrated in the world, examining the dilemmas raised by too much or not enough tourism in developing countries, and speculating about what work would be like in the future.

By the early 1980s, "over half the education authorities in the UK were promoting world studies" and many more teachers were using resources produced by aid agencies and a growing number of development education centers.[57] The successful Centre for Global Education in York even offered a diploma course in global education. In some schools, world studies incorporated aspects of peace studies, international understanding, education for world citizenship, and development studies. At other times they were taught alongside world studies. However, as Derek Heater notes, in order to promote international understanding, lessons needed to emphasize "affective rather than cognitive learning.[58] Over the course of the 1980s, the term "world studies" was gradually replaced with global education, "a more inclusive term that included the work of other vanguard educators and implied an approach rather than a single subject."[59]

The neoconservative resurgence of the 1980s also had significant consequences for English schools, but did not influence global education in the same way as the American case. Thatcher's government introduced market rationality into education through an agenda of parent choice and financial reform which rewarded successful schools at the expense of those with declining enrollment. Further, as we will see in Chapter 4, schools were asked to play a more significant role with respect to training children in skills for employability. Nevertheless, until the end of the decade the curriculum remained in the hands of teachers. Thus, the content of world studies and other courses was decided by teachers, many of whom were less than impressed with the market-rationale for schools. In England, world or global studies continued to emphasize a postnational agenda of global issues, enquiry-based learning, alternative futures, participatory learning, active learning, peace, and justice.

Conclusion

This chapter has described the different forms of international education as well as the rise of global education from the late 1960s. Clearly, very different ideas were put forward in the name of global education. For some, global education was tied to extending the power of the nation overseas: this was the case especially for an American elite asserting its authority around the world. Here, national and international goals became blurred and global education meant acquiring regional knowledge and foreign languages so that national interests could be recognized and defended. American leaders moved to fill these gaps in knowledge and ensure that the curriculum reflected the nation's new international role.

For others, the global turn signified a transition to new, postmodern world in which the threat of environmental catastrophe demanded that humanity should pull back from its Enlightenment assumptions about rationality, progress, and the search for truth. For these early global theorists, the objective of global education was to challenge prevailing attitudes toward modernity and the human condition.

What is common to global education is an "attempt to effect change in some aspect of children's education about the world,"[60] and that children's "competencies and component capacities and abilities be widely distributed within the society."[61] In seeking to influence social attitudes and political practices, global education and world studies can thus be viewed as a form of social reform. Schools have always had an important role in socializing children into society: both American and English schools promoted the values of democracy, loyalty to the nation, community participation, social well-being, and so forth. What is different about global education is that it is a movement to *change* the values of society more broadly through educating children. This point is explored further throughout the book.

During the first wave of global education, however, global ideas remained peripheral in American and English society. In the next chapter we consider the second wave of global education: that which was associated with globalization from the early 1990s. We will also discuss how far there is merit to the global society thesis.

Notes

1 Gutek (1993) p. 20.

2 Heartfield, J. "Where They Teach You How to be Thick," *Spiked-online*, March 2nd, 2011. Accessed: http://www.spiked-online.com/index.php/site/article/10254/

3 Brickman (1950) cited in Sylvester (2007) p. 11.

4 Stoker (1933) cited in Sylvester (2007) p. 17.

5 Sylvester (2007) p. 17.

6 UNESCO "Introducing UNESCO: What We Are." 2009. Accessed: http://www.unesco.org/new/en/unesco/about-us/who-we-are/introducing-unesco/

7   Malik, K. (2008) p. 158.

8   Hayden (2006) p. 10.

9   Cambridge and Thompson (2004) p.165.

10 Ibid. p. 162.

11 Gutek (1993).

12 Taba, H. & Van Til, W., *Democratic Human Relations: Promising Practices in Intergroup and Intercultural Education in the Social Studies. Sixteenth Yearbook of the National Council of Social Studies*, 1945.

13 Stephenson (1989) p. 9.

14 Reardon (1989) p. 23.

15 Ibid. p. 24.

16 Buergenthal and Torney (1976) p. 2.

17 Mackinder cited in Mayhew (2000) p. 134.

18 Zhang and Foskett (2003).

19 Standish (2009) p. 53.

20 Gutek (1993) pp. 38–9.

21 Jones and Murphy (1962).

22 Tye (1991) p. 5.

23 Tucker cited in Tye (2009) p. 7.

24 Tye (2009) p. 7.

25 Stapp *et al.* (1969).

26 Standish (2009) p. 55.

27 World Commission on Environment and Development (1987) p. 43.

28 National Governors Association, *America in Transition: The International Frontier*. Report of the Task Force on International Education, 1989.

29 Gourevitch (2007) p. 67.

30 Dicken (2003).

31 "Apollo 8: Earthrise," NASA Science Photo Library, National Space Science Data Center, 1968. Accessed: http://nssdc.gsfc.nasa.gov/photo_gallery/photogallery-earthmoon.html

32 Anderson (1979).

33 Meadows *et al.* (1972).

34 UNESCO (1974).

35 Lidstone and Stoltman (2002).

36 Cox and Scruton (1984).

37 Fisher (1985) p. 5.

38 Nesbitt, cited in Gaudelli (2003) p. 5.

39 Anderson (1979).

40 Haipt (1980) p. 7.

41 King (1976) cited in Haipt (1980) p. 7.

42 Hirsch (2006) p. 5.

43 Hanvey (1976) p. 31.

44 Midgley (2007) p. 8.

45 Fisher (1985) p. 15.

46 Office of Education (1979).

47 Alger cited in Anderson (1991) p. 126.

48 Ibid. p. 126.

49 Klein and Tye (1979) p. 209.

50 Becker (1991) p. 74.

51 Huntington (2004).

52 One World Trust cited in Heater (1982) p. 220.

53 Heater (1982) p. 219.

54 Harwood (1995).

55 Fisher (1985) p. 31.

56 Ibid. p. 87.

57 Holden (2000) p. 74.

58 Heater (1982) p. 221.

59 Holden (2000) p. 76.

60 Anderson (1979) p. 13.

61 Ibid. p. 366.

2

The making of global schools

This chapter documents the growth of global and international education initiatives in the US and England since the early 1990s. It shows how governments, the business community, academics, nonprofit organizations, and some educators have incorporated global thinking into the curriculum of schools and sometimes higher education. All of these actors are seeking moral purpose for schools in something external to education; they are engaged in global governance, profit making, global advocacy, or they are looking for a way to engage children through political issues. First, we will make some observations about the turn toward global advocacy by political leaders and academics in the post-Cold War period. This provides the context for the application of global thinking to schools. We will show how in American schools there has been a strong emphasis on the market rationale for education, while in English schools nonprofits have taken a leading role in the development of global education.

The rise of global advocacy

In brief, global advocacy means advocating for change at the international level, rather than seeking to advance national geopolitical interests. While some commentators describe the rise of the global as a gradual evolutionary process, David Chandler suggests that the 1990s marked the beginning of a qualitatively new period in international relations.[1] In the post-Cold War world, Western leaders have managed to project themselves as a force for global good, as opposed to national self-interest, through the language of universal values such as human rights, democracy, freedom, and empowerment. While there is not the space here to enter into a full discussion of this qualitative shift in mindset, the transition to global advocacy informs the recent rise of global and international education initiatives.

Chandler draws a distinction between a pre-1990 normative international human rights agenda and a post-1990 period in which human rights became institutionalized. He notes that while the 1948 UN Convention on Human Rights described human rights in the abstract and in terms of morality, in the 1990s, human rights achieved an unprecedented political and legal reality. Western intervention in Iraq (1991), Somalia (1992), Rwanda (1994), Bosnia Herzegovina (1995), Kosovo (1999), and East Timor (1999) were all justified in the language of humanitarian action. Kosovo was the first war launched in the name of human rights. In the eyes of the UK Prime Minister Tony Blair, this was a "moral crusade" fought for moral values.[2] This new approach disrupted the post-World War II political and legal framework of national sovereignty. New doctrines and institutions have been created to prosecute global advocacy. For example, in 1997, Britain announced that its foreign aid would be tied to humanitarian objectives. In 2001, the International Criminal Court was established to place on trial individuals the international community deemed in violation of its code human rights.

The idea of a global civil society has been used to theorize the globalization of politics, especially among academics and political activists on the Left.[3] In a global civil society politics is characterized by networks of governments, nonprofit or nongovernmental organizations (NGOs), religious groups, and multinational corporations all working together to address global issues. It is this amorphous network that is often referred to in the term the "international community," sometimes including heads of nation states. Mary Kaldor describes it in the following way:

> Global civil society is a platform inhabited by activists (or post-Marxists), NGOs and neo-liberals, as well as national

and religious groups, where they argue about, campaign for (or against), negotiate about, or lobby for the arrangements that shape global developments.[4]

With this network of global governance, the boundaries between state and nonstate, private and public, and military and civilian organizations have become blurred. Consequently, global governance is also characterized by blurred lines of responsibility and accountability. Networks and linkages have replaced clearly defined horizontal organizational structures. The popularity of the term "governance" rather than "government" captures the expansion of responsibility and organization.

The growth of the "third sector" on the international stage is one of the manifestations of this shift. While in the 1970s there were just a few hundred international nonprofits, by the mid-1990s there were over 29,000.[5] Significantly, more nonprofit groups were becoming directly funded by Western financial institutions, such as the World Bank, the EU, or government development agencies. While a small number of Western nonprofits continue to receive the bulk of financing, there are now thousands of Southern nonprofits that have become eligible through the UN to receive funding directly from the West. It has become common practice for nonprofits to be contracted by governments or other donor agencies to implement development projects. This practice has steered funding from donor countries away from recipient governments and toward nonprofits. Mark Duffield suggests that over half of all humanitarian aid is now being channeled through nonprofit and other organizations.[6]

As humanitarian work has become more political and long term, there has been less of a focus on short-term aid to nations and a shift toward steering countries away from endeavors associated with large-scale economic growth and toward smaller-scale, labor-intensive projects. It can be argued that there is in fact less emphasis upon the creation of material wealth *per se*. For example, Duffield comments that, through cooperative partnerships, contemporary development projects are seeking "to change whole societies and the behavior and attitudes of people within them."[7] Advocates for global change are not only changing the way they govern, but also aim to change "indigenous values and modes of organization" in developing countries.[8]

This emphasis upon different values and modes of organization and governance helps us to understand the significance of global thinking today. Rather than trying to explain the global turn a result of mystical "globalization forces" driving social and cultural change, as global theorists often do, it is better to see the ascendance of global thought as a change in the way advocates view society. This is the approach taken in this book. The transition to a global society is, therefore, a semiconscious choice by people who want to move beyond national democracies and revise institutions (including schools) to reflect a new set of postmodern values. In place of advancing the cultural and economic wealth of nations, globalists insist that we must all change our way of life in response to "global issues" of environmental degradation, malnutrition, human rights abuses, natural disasters, and so on. The turn toward global advocacy by politicians, business leaders, and academics since the end of the 1980s has been the key driver of social change.

Building American schools with a global mission

In the United States there are three principal sources of the new movement for global (or international) education: corporations, academics, and nonprofit organizations. We will begin by briefly illustrating the growth of business involvement in American education, before discussing the coalitions responsible for promoting global education.

Corporate America goes back to school

In 1990, the US Secretary of Labor, Lynn Martin, convened a blue-ribbon commission of experts to evaluate the workplace skills that would be needed in the twenty-first century, and how well American schools were equipping students with these skills. The commission reported that, "Despite sincere, well-intentioned efforts to respond, the schools – lacking clear and consistent guidance – continue with the system and methodologies they inherited from a system designed nearly 100 years ago for the needs of business organizations that are now quite different."[9] This view—that what children learn in schools needs to be more closely aligned with the needs of a now globalized economy—became more popular from the late 1980s. Experimental reform initially came in the form of the standards movement, school vouchers, and charter schools. Gradually, the language of business was applied to public education: choice, performance, accountability, measurement, competition, and privatization. The measurement and accountability agenda for schools was passed into law through the 2001 No Child Left Behind Act. By now corporate America was taking a new role in public education. Whereas generous financial support for education initiatives was nothing new, new foundations backed by Big Business "wanted nothing less than to transform American education," suggests Diane Ravitch.[10] In her book, *The Death and Life of the Great American School System*, Ravitch details the new business model of schooling that would come to dominate some public school systems in the 2000s. Ravitch identifies three of the largest foundations to have played a leading role in educational reform: the Bill and Melinda Gates Foundation, the Walton Family Foundation, and the Eli and Edythe Broad Foundation. Of these, Ravitch argues that the Gates Foundation has cast such a wide and deep web of funding to think-tanks and advocacy groups that it has left "almost no one willing to criticize its vast power and unchecked influence."[11] For instance, the Gates Foundation has provided some $100 million to charter school managers and another $100 million to create two hundred new small high schools in New York City.

In particular, charter schools have been used to introduce certain reforms to public education through the back door. Practices that are not accepted in public schools because of teaching unions have been implemented in charter schools, including nonunionized labor, merit pay, and an end to tenure. The success of charter schools and New York's small high schools has been mixed, to say the least.[12]

The new prominence of corporate leaders in directing school reform should not necessarily be viewed as the success of a Right-wing, neoliberal agenda. Rather, reform has taken a more pragmatic character, with politicians and education leaders promising to implement "whatever works," frequently welcoming the resources and attention of business leaders. In New York City, Michael Bloomberg's "schools' revolution" is a case in point. From his election in 2001, Bloomberg adopted a top-down, business-style management of the city's schools, distancing himself and his colleagues from ideological positions. He quickly abolished the influential Board of Education and hired management consultants and business leaders as advisors. Lawyer Joel Klein was appointed schools chancellor for much of the decade (in 2010 he was replaced by magazine CEO Catherine Black, who lasted just three months in the position). Bloomberg utilized the Leadership Academy for training would-be principals in business management techniques. In doing so, management skills were elevated above a background in education and teaching as the requisite training for leading a school. Bloomberg imposed "evidence-based" literacy and mathematics programs on schools and teachers, who were given little choice in how these would be taught. These included both phonics to teach reading and constructivist mathematics (where children build their own mathematical concepts). The teaching of phonics has historically been associated with the Right, while child-centered constructivism came from the Left; this fairly arbitrary selection of methodologies illustrates the administration's pragmatic approach.

Bloomberg's and Klein's commitment to "whatever works" arises not from a principled vision of education, but rather the opposite. Later in his term, Bloomberg allowed some schools more freedom to teach as they saw fit, but only in return for agreeing to set targets for improvement on tests. As Nick Frayn observes:

> Without a more substantial vision as to the underlying ends of education, the Bloomberg administration has become fixated on the means of administering education. This has led to a damaging fixation on accountability, as well as a problematic search for a measurable definition of what constitutes success and failure in education.[13]

Education can only be successful when one has a clear understanding of its purpose, which in turn is connected to how we perceive ourselves as social beings. The pragmatic approach taken by Bloomberg's administration, as well as others, "reduced teaching to test preparation."[14] Here, education becomes little more than mastering literacy and numeracy skills for use in the workplace. Unfortunately, as we will see in Chapter 4, this model of "education" actually inhibits the preparation of young people for the demands of work.

What we have seen in New York, and in other cities, is the extension of the economic rationale for education into the everyday management and practices of schools. No longer is the employability skills agenda a matter of rhetoric. Schools are almost becoming an extension of the corporate world, redesigned in its image. As Bill Gates explained in an address to the nation's governors, "Our high schools were designed to meet the needs of another age."[15] In his view, learning should be directly related to the lives and goals of children. What Gates and others mean is that schools should be teaching only knowledge and skills that will be used by people in their everyday lives. In their minds, educating children about the world, whether relevant or not, is of "another age."

Coalition building

Global education has been promoted by a number of nonprofit groups and also institutions of higher education. While corporations tend to focus on skills for the workplace, nonprofits, universities, and colleges are more likely to emphasize social skills and values associated with global citizenship. Nevertheless, many of these groups have created a space for themselves to work together and promote their vision of schooling under the heading of global or international education.

There are a number of centers at colleges and universities producing global education materials, training teachers in global education, or working on collaborative projects with schools. For instance, the University of Illinois at Urbana Champaign runs a Center for Global Studies, which publishes articles and resource materials about global education for K-12 teachers; the Midwest Institute for International/Intercultural Education, Oshtemo, Missouri, is a self-funded consortium of two-year colleges located in the region that have been working to support curriculum and professional development along global lines; Rutgers University has a Global Citizen 2000 project through which it cooperates with local schools; Rice University, New York, offers an online teacher education program in global education; and the University of South Florida is developing a Global Citizenship general education program in its School for Global Sustainability. This latter initiative has been supported by the Association of American Colleges and

Universities, which operates a project titled "Shared Futures: Global Learning and Social Responsibility." Some universities and colleges also advocate a global approach to education for their own institutions. Farleigh Dickenson University in New Jersey aims to nurture global citizens as described in its Global Education Strategic Plan: "The University strives to provide students with the multidisciplinary, intercultural and ethical understandings necessary to participate, lead and prosper in the global marketplace of ideas, commerce and culture."[16] At other institutions of higher education, however, global education or global citizenship may be mentioned in passing, but have had little consequence in terms of curricular study. A number of colleges and universities, such as George Mason University, have centers for global education which simply organize study abroad programs.

Again, there are significant differences between programs and institutions in terms of approach to global or international education. However, we can distinguish between those that are seeking to enhance knowledge and understanding of the world, and those who have embraced other aims for education. So, while there are many established National Resource Centers for Foreign Language, Area Studies and International Studies that fall into the former category, many new initiatives view global education differently. For instance, the Global Citizenship general education program at the University of South Florida aims to "cultivate engaged global citizens skilled in problem solving, attentive to human diversity and cultural complexity, and instilled with a sense of personal and social responsibility."[17] What differentiates many of these new programs is that they aim to cultivate certain skills and promote a particular view of the world instead of grounding students in disciplinary knowledge, regional knowledge, or a foreign language. Thus, South Florida's Global Citizenship program "incorporates principles inherent in social and environmental sustainability."[18]

Some of the nonprofit groups that have been actively promoting global education include the World Affairs Council, the Council for Global Education, the American Forum for Global Education, the Longview Foundation, the Model United Nations program, the Center for the Advancement and Study of International Education, Global Citizens for Change, Global Education Associates in New York, the Boston Research Centre for the 21st Century, and the Global Education Advisory Council in Massachusetts. The Council for Global Education (CGE) explains its mission thus:

The goal of the CGE is to create a world where values such as peace, coexistence, reverence for all forms of life, and responsibility are the norm. Needed is a new education based on new goals for a new and enlightened century. To achieve this goal, CGE has developed a global education model founded upon: Universal Values, Global Understanding, Excellence in All Things, and Service to Humanity.[19]

While all of these nonprofits have been active contributors to the movement for global education, it is the Asia Society that has been leading a national coalition involving national education institutions, policy makers, and business leaders. The Asia Society is a nonprofit educational organization whose original aim was simply to improve the connections between Asian people and the US. However, its website highlights a broader rationale for international education:

From science and culture to sports and politics, ideas and capital are crossing borders and spanning the world. The globalization of business, the advances in technology, and the acceleration of migration increasingly require the ability to work on a global scale. As a result of this new connectivity, our high school graduates will need to be far more knowledgeable about world regions and global issues, and able to communicate across cultures and languages.[20]

In this example, it is evident that the starting point for those who want to "internationalize" the curriculum is their perception of social, political, economic, or environmental problems. Their approach to education is to see it as a means to address the real world problems that preoccupy (adult) society, rather than asking, "what are the important knowledge and skills that children need to learn in school such that they become educated individuals?"

Coordinated by the Asia Society, the National Coalition on Asia and International Studies in Schools comprises over thirty organizations and companies including the President of the American

Federation of Teachers, the President of the National Education Association, the President and CEO of the American Association of Colleges for Teacher Education, the Executive Director of the National Association for Secondary School Principals, and representatives from the National Council for Social Studies, the National School Boards Association, the National Geographic Society, the Longview Foundation, the Bill and Melinda Gates Foundation, and the Goldman Sachs Foundation. The coalition aims to promote the importance of international education, to build political momentum for change, and to encourage schools to embrace international education.[21]

As was noted in the previous chapter, international education and global education have evolved differently and reflect different approaches to education. Yet in recent years, many educators have been using the terms interchangeably and indeed, many of the contemporary initiatives to internationalize the curriculum are indistinguishable from global education in terms of content and aims. What characterizes both is an emphasis upon solving issues, interpersonal communication, values, and vocational skills rather than mastery of subject-based knowledge. Part of the reason for the more popular use of the term "international education" in the US today is no doubt connected to the derisory criticism that global education received in previous decades.[22] Nevertheless, the introduction of recent international education programs has not been without controversy either, as will be discussed below.

Human Rights Education mirrors and contributes to many of the themes of global education. The years 1995–2004 were designated as the "United Nations Decade for Human Rights Education," and there is some evidence of its inclusion in US curricula. A survey conducted in 2001 found that twenty states included human rights content in state-level curriculum documents, social studies standards, or assessment documents, while others had plans to do so.[23] Human Rights Education is advocated by the Human Rights Resource Centre at the University of Minnesota, which has been running a Human Rights Education Experience in conjunction with the Minnesota Department for Human Rights. In addition to human rights, the project titled "This is My Home" teaches students about issues of social justice, democracy, responsibility, and interdependence. Another example comes from Hunterdon Central High School in Flemington, New Jersey, which offers a curriculum for global citizenship where students learn about efforts to establish human rights and about state-sponsored violations of human rights.[24]

State-wide initiatives

Since 2001, the Asia Society's coalition has been encouraging states to incorporate international education into their curricula, offering professional development in international education to teachers, and promoting ways in which schools can become more internationally orientated. This has been most successful when states have built their own coalitions for international education. With financial backing from the Longview Foundation, the Goldman Sachs Corporation, and the Bill and Melinda Gates Foundation, the Asia Society has been supporting initiatives in 25 states (Figure 2). This is not an exhaustive map of international education in the US as some states are developing their own programs, Massachusetts being one example. A pattern repeated in a number of states is that education departments appoint a task force to survey current curricula and attitudes toward international education. This is followed by a

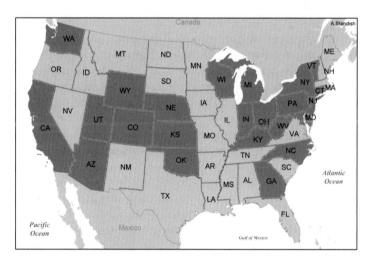

FIGURE 2 Map of US States Adopting International Education.

(Source: Asia Society, http://asiasociety.org/node/20794)

state-wide conference or summit attracting educators from K-12 and higher education, business leaders, policy makers, and state officials. A strategy is then drawn up to promote international education across the state, to modify state standards to include international education, to establish links between local and international schools, and to train teachers in the benefits of international education. For many states, this has been taking place over the past decade. Here, we will describe initiatives in Wisconsin, New Jersey, and North Carolina, three states that have made significant inroads toward incorporating global aims in their curricula.

Wisconsin was the first state to appoint an international education coordinator and it subsequently pioneered a curriculum-planning guide, *Planning Curriculum in International Education*. The guide has since become a national resource for teachers and policy makers. The Wisconsin Department of Instruction organized a series of workshops to train teachers in how to infuse all eleven subject areas with global content and it has set up agreements with schools in France, Germany, Japan, and Thailand for pupil and teacher exchange. Wisconsin's objectives for enhanced international education in the state are set out in the document *Strategies for Achieving Global Literacy for Wisconsin Students*. These include a State-wide International Education Council to support biennial International Education Summits; five Regional Leadership Alliances; teacher and administrator development (encouraging teachers to learn a language, teach abroad, and attend workshops on integrating global perspectives); providing pupils with opportunities to read world literature, learn artistic and musical traditions of other cultures, address transnational environmental problems, and travel abroad; and encouraging every school to have a sister school abroad.

New Jersey's first International Education Summit was held in October of 2004 at Princeton University, bringing together over 300 educators, policy makers, and business representatives. The summit report highlighted three goals, including enhancing teacher capacity for international teaching and connecting international education to real-world experiences for children. The final goal illustrates just how profound a change in the orientation of schools was being proposed:

To help students understand, connect to and act on critical global issues by integrating international perspectives into curricula in all core curriculum content standards areas with special emphasis on . . . world languages instruction . . . .social studies instruction that focuses on global issues.[25]

This represents a complete re-orientation in the approach to teaching across the entire curriculum. At one of the follow-up teacher training conferences, workshops were held explaining how different subject areas, including English, science, and mathematics, could all be taught through an international lens.

In 2006, the New Jersey Department for Education revised its K-12 social studies standards to include an international focus. A new strand, International Education, was added to the civics standards, with the rationale that, "International education enables students to broaden their understanding of global issues that impact their life as Americans."[26] For instance, at grade eight it is suggested that pupils, "Discuss how global challenges are interrelated, complex, and changing and that even local issues have a global dimension (e.g. environmental issues, transportation)."[27] At grade 12 pupils are expected to be able to, "Connect the concept of universal human rights to world events and issues."[28] It is worth recalling that the United States has not signed the Universal Declaration on Human Rights at this point in time: yet the authors of the standards included this concept without any reference to how it might conflict with rights defined at the national level in the civics strand. A broader revision of six curriculum content areas was completed in 2009. This included the integration of twenty-first century skills and themes, global perspectives, technology, and interdisciplinary connections.[29]

The University of North Carolina's Center for International Understanding and the governor's office have been promoting international education for several years through a project called "North Carolina in the World." In 2003, this initiative received the Goldman Sachs Prize for International Education in the state category. North Carolina's action plan for international education lists five goals, one of which is increasing teachers' knowledge about the world. A study group was established to formulate objectives and strategies for strengthening preservice teachers' world knowledge. It is worth noting one of the findings of the study group reported by Assistant Professor Adam Friedman: "The data gathered from this survey suggest that Global Education and Awareness is regarded by deans of colleges of education within North Carolina as a critical topic in terms of preparing undergraduate pre-service teachers."[30] The findings and recommendations of the study group were published in the report *North Carolina in the World: Preparing North Carolina Teachers for an Interconnected World*. The document is introduced with the question, posed by Erskine Bowles, President of the University: "How do we instill a global perspective in our teacher education candidates, thereby building their capacity to prepare students to interact with the world community both inside and outside North Carolina's borders?"[31] The report lists the following recommendations for the preparation of teacher candidates: more participation in structured international experiences including study abroad, more interactions with international universities and K-12 students, cultural experiences within the community, the completion of more internationally focused coursework including language study, and collaboration with university students abroad. For its teacher education faculty the report recommends focused faculty development activities including travel abroad, partnerships with international studies and international program colleagues, and collaborative projects with international colleagues, including coteaching.

There is of course much valuable knowledge and insight that can be gained from building international connections and studying other cultures. In lessons where teachers are following an international or global approach, the pupils are often engaged with learning about different countries, people, their history, and the challenges people face. This happens partially because of a gap between the lofty ambitions of advocates for global education and the reality of the need to engage children with content in the classroom. However, this does not change the fact that the current movement for global or international education is seeking to replace an education in subject knowledge with other aims including "awareness" of global issues, "skills" of communication, and recognition of alternative "perspectives"; the outcome of which is a more superficial engagement with knowledge.

National initiatives

An international or global dimension to the curriculum is identified by a number of national organizations in the US. For example, the National Council for Social Studies includes Global Connections as one of ten themes for social studies because, "Students will need to be able to address such international issues as health care, the environment, human rights, economic competition and interdependence, age-old ethnic enmities, and political and military alliances."[32] Similarly, the National Council for the Accreditation of Teacher Education includes the ability to teach from "multicultural and global perspectives" as Standard IV of their Standards for Professional Development Schools.[33]

Over the past few years, momentum has been building in support of the Partnership for 21st Century Skills (P21). This public–private coalition was formed in 2002 and aims to "modernize" education by incorporating "twenty-first century skills" into the curriculum in every state.[34] The approximately thirty-five members of the partnership include Adobe Systems, American Association of School Libraries, Apple, Blackboard Inc., Cisco Systems, Dell Inc., the Education Network of America, Education Testing Service, Hewlett Packard, Intel Foundation, Knowledge Works Foundation, Lenovo, McGraw-Hill, Microsoft Corporation, National Education Association, Scholastic Education, Verizon, and Walt Disney Company. While one might expect the National Education Association to play a role in curriculum reform, what is surprising about this list is that most of these organizations provide a service for schools, while others have very little whatsoever to do with schools. This means that instead of responding to the needs of teachers publishers, technology providers, testing services, and other resource providers are now seeking to drive curriculum reform themselves.

By the end of 2010, P21 had been adopted and incorporated into the standards of nineteen states. While this initiative does not directly identify with global education, it shares some common assumptions about education, especially the desire to replace subject knowledge with a skills-based curriculum. Among the skills the partnership proposes as more "relevant" for today's children are critical thinking, global awareness, civic literacy, communication skills, and leadership. These "global skills" are the subject of Chapter 4, where they will be explored in greater detail. Nevertheless, at the time of writing, it looks as though P21 may well be superseded by another skills initiative.

In June 2010, the National Governors Association (NGA) and the Council of Chief State School Officers (CCSSO) jointly released their *Common Core State Standards for English Language Arts and Mathematics*, the aim of which is to prepare children for a "global economy and society."[35] Emphasizing the lack of federal involvement, their standards were produced in consultation with teachers, school administrators, and "experts." Thus far, the *Common Core State Standards* have received widespread support, being adopted by forty-five states. Whereas P21 was criticized for being dismissive of disciplines, the *Common Core State Standards* break subjects down into skills sets. It is also becoming clear that there has been collaboration between these two initiatives. While Microsoft was one of the founding members of P21, the NGA and CCSSO both received significant backing from the Bill and Melinda Gates Foundation in the form of millions of dollars to support the writing of the standards.[36] The Gates Foundation has also financed two nonprofit organizations: Achieve Inc., to write tests aligned to the *Common Core State Standards*, and the Alliance for Excellent Education, to "grow support" for the standards.[37]

Another way in which some schools have added an international dimension to their curriculum is through the International Baccalaureate (IB). The first IB Diploma Program in the US was authorized in 1971 at the United Nations International School, a private school in New York. In 1998, the first IB Primary Years Program was offered at the Dwight School, also a private school in New York. By 1999 there were 300 schools offering either, the Primary Years Program, the Middle Years Program, or the Diploma Program (High School).[38] In 2011, this figure was approaching 1,300 (approximately 90 per cent of which are state schools). The majority of these schools were offering the Diploma Program either alongside or in place of Advanced Placement (AP) courses. Like AP, the IB Diploma is now recognized for college-level credit by some 800 American universities.[39] Schools that have taken on an international or global approach to education tend to be those where there are teachers who are motivated by its ideals: for example, the International Magnet School for Global Citizenship in Connecticut or the Mariposa Elementary School of Global Education in California.

The growing acceptance of the IB Diploma in higher education is partly a reflection of its positive academic standing,[40] but is also connected to its internationalist perspective. In the US, the growth of IB World Schools has not been without controversy. In a number of states, including Utah, Michigan, Idaho, Pennsylvania, and New Hampshire, parents have protested against the IB because they see it as un-American, anti-Christian, socialist, and promoting the values of the United Nations (environmentalism, human rights, conflict resolution).[41] The problem is not with the academic quality of IB, rather it is perceived as in conflict with the values of American communities because it does not reflect their worldview. As one exasperated parent explained: "They want to change the way your child thinks, not feed your child's mind with information, and information about our history, heritage and why we believe what we believe."[42] The International Baccalaureate Organization is a part of the Economic and Social Council of the United Nations, and IB programs were initially designed for children of parents working for the United Nations or other families working abroad. It should therefore come as no surprise that the IB programs reflect the values of the United Nations. It should also be no surprise that these values may well conflict with those of some American communities. These communities were not part of its creation, and its courses are not designed with them in mind.

There are clearly a number of different educational initiatives being promoted for American schools under the heading of global education and/or international education. As a general rule (to which there are no doubt some exceptions), the more established international education programs, such as National Research Centers and International schools, are more likely to teach subject knowledge, while newer initiatives tend to emphasize vocational skills, academic skills, personal skills, and espouse "global" values. What the latter group holds in common is a desire to move education away from subject knowledge and American traditions toward their new, global vision for education.

Global education in England

Curriculum patterns in schools are somewhat different in England. Development education and environmental education have been promoted in England by an array of nonprofit groups for over thirty years, and hence it is these organizations which have been most influential in shaping the form of global education in schools.[43] Yet until the new millennium the place of development education was confined to those schools where it was supported by teachers and its place in the national curriculum was marginal. Nevertheless, change was afoot. As one practitioner reported, "Suddenly development education isn't on the fringe – it is mainstream."[44] The remainder of this chapter will explore how this transition came about.

In England, as in the US, the thawing of the Cold War pulled the rug from under the feet of the political Right. Political leaders struggled to offer a coherent view of national culture and ideals in the absence of competition with the Soviet Union. In this context global advocacy emerged as a potential new source of authority. With the narrowing parameters of national politics, education became focused on areas of personal "relevance" to children: personal, social, health, and vocational education. This is the political context in which global education has thrived: through global education, schools began encouraging children to develop a sense of identity in relation to global issues and the global market.

The 1990s was a decade of transition for British education. It began with the launching of a subject-based national curriculum by a Conservative government under Prime Minister John Major (1990–97), and ended with the introduction of personal, social and health education, as well as global citizenship education, by the New Labour government under Tony Blair (1997–2007). But despite initial contradictory appearances, there was a significant continuity in the transition from the Major to the Blair regimes. The question of citizenship was investigated by the House of Commons Speaker's Commission on Education (1990), the National Curriculum Council (1990), the Commission on Social Justice (1994), and the Citizenship Foundation (1995). Following the 1997 White Paper *Excellence in Schools*, the Advisory Group on Citizenship was formed to make recommendations for the introduction of a citizenship curriculum. Under the leadership of Bernard Crick, the report led to a mandatory citizenship curriculum for primary and secondary pupils in which citizenship was presented as existing on a continuum from local to national to global. This was no traditional citizenship curriculum offering lessons in civics and national history: while the British political system and culture was included, much of the content was orientated toward an exploration of personal values, identity, and behavior, taught across all subjects from geography, to English, and physical education.[45]

Discussion of globalization and a global civil society also changed the nonprofit/nongovernmental sector. During the 1990s there was greater coordination of nonprofit organizations and a consolidation of development education traditions under the heading of global education.[46] Thus, proponents of human rights education, environmental education, education for sustainable development, antiracist education, world studies, and development education found common ground under the umbrella concept of "global education" or sometimes "global citizenship education."

One of the more influential nonprofits promoting global education has been Oxfam. In 1997 Oxfam launched *A Curriculum for Global Citizenship*, promoting as its vision of a global citizen someone who:

Is aware of the wider world and has a sense of their own role as a world citizen; respects and values diversity; has an understanding of the how the world works economically, politically, socially, culturally, technologically, and environmentally; is outraged by social injustice; participates in and contributes to the community at a range of levels from the local to the global; is willing to act to make the world a more sustainable place; takes responsibility for their actions.[47]

Updated in 2002, Oxfam's curriculum has been used and cited by educators far and wide, including in the US. Its themes have frequently been usurped by policy documents on global citizenship. Other influential nonprofit organizations who have been busily producing global education teaching material include ActionAid, the British Council, Catholic Agency for Overseas Development (CAFOD), Christian Action Research and Education (CARE), the Central Bureau for International Education and Training, Christian Aid, the Commonwealth Institute, the Council for Environmental Education, the Council for Education in World Citizenship, the Development Education Association, the Nuffield Foundation, Practical Action, Voluntary Services Overseas (VSO), and the World Wildlife Fund (WWF). In all, there are over fifty nonprofit groups contributing to global education in English schools, and a further forty development education centers doing likewise.

In their report *Global Dimension in Secondary Schools*, Douglas Bourn and Frances Hunt note that nonprofit groups are "often the first point of contact in bringing a development or global issue into the school."[48] While the government can publish documents, nonprofits are frequently the ones on the ground providing teachers with classroom materials and training. Oxfam itself works directly with some 3,000 primary and secondary schools, while Practical Action has direct links with 2,500 schools.[49]

As noted above, the standing and influence of nonprofit groups has been significantly elevated through their assimilation with the government's development aims and initiatives. The amalgamation of the statutory and voluntary sectors has occurred in education as it has in foreign policy. Early in the new century, several new documents promoting global education for schools were jointly produced by government agencies and nonprofit groups. *Developing the Global Dimension in the School Curriculum* was aimed at head teachers, governors, senior managers, local education authorities, teachers, and early-years practitioners. Initially published in 2000, the report asserted that the global dimension enabled links to be made between local and global issues so that young people are given opportunities to:

> [C]ritically examine their own values and attitudes; appreciate the similarities and differences between people everywhere; and value diversity; understand the global context of their local lives; and develop skills that will enable them to combat injustice, prejudice and discrimination. Such knowledge, skills and understanding enables young people to make informed decisions about playing an active role in the global community.[50]

Those contributing to the writing of this document included Oxfam, the Centre for Global Education, Christian Aid, the Council for Education in World Citizenship, Tourism Concern, a number of regional development education centers, and several schools. The publication highlights the following key concepts as the "core of learning" about global issues: citizenship, sustainable development, social justice, values and perceptions, diversity, interdependence, conflict resolution, and human rights, all plucked from Oxfam's global citizenship curriculum.

Developing the Global Dimension in the School Curriculum was followed by two documents, *A Framework for the International Dimension for Schools in England*, produced by The Central Bureau for International Education and Training and the Development Education Association, and *Citizenship Education: The Global Dimension*. The former provided guidance for incorporating "sustainability, the environment, global interdependence, cultural diversity, preparation for adult life and citizenship education" into the revised national curriculum in order to "reflect modern day realities."[51] The latter was designed to help secondary schools as the new citizenship curriculum came into effect in 2002: it was published by the Development Education Association (DEA) and written by a consortium consisting of the Central Bureau for International Education and Training, the Commonwealth Institute, the Council for Environmental Education, the Council for Education in World Citizenship, and Oxfam, with the support of the Department for Education and Employment and the Department for International Development (DfID).[52]

The DEA began as a national network in the 1980s. In 1997, the organization was expanded with financial support coming from the newly formed DfID. The DEA has since taken a leading role in the promotion and implementation of global education and in 2011 assumed the new title and identity "Think Global." It hosts the "Global Dimensions" website, which includes links to the above government-sponsored global education documents, information on how to integrate global education into the national curriculum, global education resources for each subject discipline, information about training in global education, and contact details for development education centers across England. The DEA has also worked with subject associations to produce guidelines on how each subject contributes to global education. For instance, *Geography: The Global Dimension* was jointly written with the Geographical Association.[53] Again, it takes Oxfam's eight core global education concepts and shows how each can be addressed through the teaching of geography. Perhaps more than most subjects, geography has embraced the themes of global education/citizenship and education for sustainable development in place of teaching children about the geography of the world.

DfID has become the main link between the government and nonprofits, and a key source of funding. Commencing in 2000, the Partnership Program Arrangement provided £90 million (approximately $140 million) per year to support large UK-based organizations.[54] Over the past decade many nonprofits have benefits from this funding source including ActionAid, CAFOD, CARE, Christian Aid, Oxfam, the International HIV/AIDS Alliance, One World Action, the International Institute for Environment and Development, VSO, and WWF. DfID has been committed to embedding global issues in the school curriculum through its program Enabling Effective Support, which was launched in 2000. Working in conjunction with the DEA, funding was provided to establish twelve regional networks, each with their own coordinator responsible for furnishing teachers with the tools and skills to teach global issues.

Regional development education centers have been a key part of this network. For instance, covering Berkshire, the Reading International Solidarity Centre (RISC) began life as World Education Berkshire in 1981. In 1994, it moved into an impressive three-storey listed building on London Street in downtown Reading; today, it houses a shop, a development education resource library with over 7,000 titles, offices, a cafe, and a roof-top garden. It is funded through its shop, its membership, donations, and grants from Oxfam, Christian Aid, Reading Borough Council, the European Union, DfID, and the National Lottery. RISC has a network of six "global schools" for which it provides curricula materials, workshops, resources, and guidance. However, through its training, workshops, and publications, it reaches hundreds more teachers. RISC's global schools embrace the global dimension as a whole-school ethos and encourage pupils to identify themselves as global citizens through an appreciation of different cultures and taking responsibility for global issues, which are embedded in the curriculum. Schools are encouraged to draw upon cultural diversity in their own communities to learn about different traditions, languages, and festivals.

The Global Schools Partnership is another program run by DfID, with the support of the British Council, Cambridge Education Foundation, UK One World Linking Association, and VSO. It provides support and funding to schools looking to make connections with schools in developing countries so that they can communicate with and learn from each other, as well as plan work around global themes and issues. DfID aims to have 5,000 UK schools participating by 2012.[55] DfID also runs an annual global student forum, which organizes volunteering and commissions research on development education and global education.

Other development education centers have been promoting their own programs for global schooling. The Developing Citizenship Project (2002–05) was jointly run by Oxfam, Save the Children, UNICEF UK, Cheshire Development Education Center, Manchester Development Education Project, Norfolk Education and Action for Development, and five education authorities. This project aimed to "see how the global dimension could become embedded in secondary schools and lead to whole-school approaches to develop Global Citizenship in: The Curriculum . . . , (the) School Ethos . . . and Active Citizenship."[56] The Global Schools (UK) Project (2005–08) was managed by Leeds Development Education Center, the Centre for Global and Development Education, and Norfolk Education and Action for Development. It supported thirty secondary schools and trained teachers and "Global Dimension coordinators" in development education issues, methodology, and incorporation of global dimension into existing schemes of work. Leeds Development Education Center also has a project to raise global awareness in primary schools called "Entitlement and Enrichment." Liverpool World Centre combined its two main initiatives, the Fair Trade Schools Project and the Climate Conscious Schools Project, under the title "Global Conscious Citizens." One of the project's aims is to involve children themselves in decisions about how the schools will address global issues, and this is done through school councils. Based in Tower Hamlets, London, the Humanities Education Centre runs several projects through its website, including Steps to a Sustainable Future, BanglaBangla, which connects local Bangladeshis with people in Bangladesh, and Story Tents, a literacy resource through which children learn about the primitive shelters that are home for many people in developing countries.[57]

Another way to get schools on board with global awareness has been the creation of awards or benchmarking for schools that have jumped through certain hoops to integrate a global dimension. Administered by the British Council, the International Schools Award has been presented to over 10,000 schools since 1999 for generating a whole-school international ethos, working with partner schools and the community, involving pupils in international work, and year-round international activity (British Council 2011). There are also awards for "Fairtrade Schools" (Fairtrade Foundation), "Eco-Schools" (Foundation for Environmental Education), "Sustainable

Schools" (Department for Children Schools and Families), "Rights Respecting Schools" (UNICEF), "Global Schools" (RISC and Yorkshire and Humber Global Schools Association), and "A Global Citizenship Audit" (Oxfam). In the main, schools integrate the global dimension through subject teaching, assemblies, special days and weeks, international links, curriculum projects, by directly contributing to a campaign run by a nonprofit, after-school clubs, and award schemes.[58]

In some cases, development education centers have also been working with colleges and universities that offer initial teacher training, such that student teachers and teacher trainers are versed in global education. In 2004, the Global Citizenship Initial Teacher Training scheme was jointly established by London and the South East Region's Global Dimension (LaSER) and the Center for Cross Curricular Initiatives at London South Bank University, with support from DfID. The scheme aimed to integrate global citizenship into the curriculum content of initial teacher training.[59] Three institutions cooperated in the project: St Mary's University College, the University of Reading, and the Institute of Education, London. In the first instance, education coordinators from local development education centers ran a series of workshops for student teachers and lecturers at the participating college or university. Each institution undertook a curricula project in local schools based on a global citizenship theme or concept, such as sustainability, conflict resolution, interdependence, or respecting diversity. At the end of the first year a day was organized for each group to present their work to an audience of students, teachers, and lecturers. In the project's second year, a follow-up activity was planned with current and new student teachers.

Here, we can see the collaboration of development education centers with institutions of education to effect change in the philosophy and teaching of local schools. Thus, in the case of Berkshire's Global Schools network, RISC and Reading University worked together to shape global education in these schools.

RISC has also worked with Westminster Institute of Education, at Oxford Brookes University. Here, it has provided seminars on global citizenship and global dimensions to four-year and postgraduate student teachers. RISC has worked with some of the faculty at Oxford Brookes to help them plan globally orientated projects, such as an art project inspired by RISC's collection of contemporary

Ghanaian artist Owusu Ankomah.[60] In Kent, Canterbury Christ Church University College has been working with the local World Education Development Group (WEDG) to integrate global education into its teacher education program. WEDG has provided workshops and resources for student teachers and lecturers, a course on the global dimension and the role of fund-raising in schools for religious education students, and has contributed to a new compulsory fourteen-week module for Bachelor of Education Year 3 students, called "Learning in the Global Context." The module highlights the theme of global connections, covering a range of global issues, including taking care of the planet. Bournemouth University's Center for Global Perspectives is another location that has contributed to global education research and teaching in both schools and the university itself. The center has three foci of activity: scholarship (development of curricula and the student experience to enhance global employability and research), creating a hub (alliances inside and outside of Bournemouth University), and engaging with business.[61]

In order to coordinate the work of global education in teacher preparation, the Centre for Cross Curricular Initiatives at London South Bank University launched the "Initial Teacher Education Network for Education for Sustainable Development/Global Citizenship" in July 2007. The network hosts a website for resource exchange and presently holds an annual conference for global educators. They are supported and funded by ESCalate, the WWF, Oxfam, and the Training and Development Agency for Schools. The network is also affiliated with UNESCO's International Teacher Education Network.

Examination boards and publishers have responded to the rising demand for global education by including global issues, global concepts, and global citizenship in syllabi and textbooks. For instance, Hodder Education in alliance with different examination boards has published *Local and Global Citizenship for CCEA GCSE—Learning for Life and Work*[62], *Key Stage 3 Workbook: Media and the Global Dimension*[63] and *A2 Geography Edexcel (B) Unit 4: Global Challenge (Population and the Economy)*.[64] As in the US, the International Baccalaureate programs and examinations have been growing in popularity. Until recently, the IB was mostly confined to private schools. In 2006, the government announced that funding was being made available so that any pupil in the state sector could opt to take an IB diploma.[65] In 2011, the IB Schools and Colleges Association lists one hundred and forty-six IB schools and colleges across England and Wales.[66] The growing popularity of IB may well also be a consequence of declining faith in Advanced Level examinations (A Level), as grade inflation has eroded their reputation as the "gold standard."

While the emphasis thus far has been placed upon the influence of those coming from a development education tradition, it is also important to recognize the input of the business community to global education in England. As in the US, international economic integration and globalization is a cornerstone of England PLC. Most business leaders want to employee young people who are orientated toward the European and global markets, rather than solely a domestic one. Thus, in the influential government report *Putting the World into World-Class Education*, New Labour's Education Secretary Charles Clarke surmised that "One cannot truly educate young people in this country without the international dimension being a very significant and real part of their learning experience."[67] In contrast to reports focused on global dimensions or global citizenship, this document viewed global education as contributing to the economic wealth of the country. Its three primary goals were:

Goal 1: Equipping our children, young people and adults for life in a global society and work in a global economy.

Goal 2: Engaging with our international partners to achieve their goals and ours.

Goal 3: Maximizing the contribution of our education and training sector and university research to overseas trade and inward investment.[68]

This different slant reflects the report's contributing organizations: the Department for Trade and Enterprise, UK Trade and Investment, the Department for Work and Pensions, the Foreign and Commonwealth Office, the British Council, DfID, and the Department for Culture, Media and Sport. Because the idea of global education is so broad, it is possible for such an array of organizations to carve their own niche under its umbrella.

In England, the discussion of a "skills gap" and the need to retrain the workforce through education dates back to the 1970s.

The details of vocational reforms to education are explored in Chapter 4. Here, it is important to note that since the early 1990s the form that this debate has taken is to address the skills needed for young people to remain competitive in a global market. Thus, the framing of global education in schools has been shaped by this economic discussion as well as the ethical dimensions inherent to development education. However, in contrast to the US, there has been little integration of these two spheres. Representatives of industry and those of development organizations have been undertaking their own initiatives to influence education for some time. The most significant recent change is the government's embrace of the personal ethics associated with global citizenship education.

In their report *Global Dimension in Secondary Schools*, Bourn and Hunt found that "there is considerable variation in the ways in which the term 'global dimension' is perceived and articulated," and that, "Schools tend to personalize their interpretation and do not directly follow national guidelines."[69] Some teachers see global education as knowledge-based, while other emphasize the skill elements or take a values-based approach. However, when asked how they saw the global dimension, teachers responded in terms of global social responsibility, world citizenship, global interconnectedness, teaching about global issues, understanding the impact of our action, understanding the bigger picture and their place within it, sustaining international links, and helping students to link their complex and different identities.[70] Evidently, with global education in England, "many schools see its focus primarily in the more moral and affective areas."[71]

In the May 2010 national election, New Labour was replaced and a new coalition government was formed between the Conservative and the Liberal Democrat parties. The Conservatives in particular have promised a review of the national curriculum and a return to core subject knowledge. The government's White Paper (2010) *The Importance of Teaching* specified that a key aim of the review was "reducing prescription and allowing schools to decide how to teach, while refocusing on the core subject knowledge that every child and young person should gain at each stage of their education."[72] Hence, it appears that the current government may want to take education in a different direction. The only references to the "global" in the White Paper are two quotations from Arne Duncan about the importance of education for the knowledge economy and maintaining competitiveness and prosperity. However, it is unlikely that the government has the authority to reverse the global turn in English schools, at least not in the short term. The influence of nonprofits inside schools is likely to remain considerable, especially given the Coalition's emphasis upon involving the institutions of civil society in activities formally organized by the State, as part of its "Big Society" agenda. At this point in time, the shape of the new national curriculum and its impact on schools when it is released in 2012–13 are uncertain.

Conclusion

This chapter has illustrated how, through the rhetoric of global change, the voluntary and corporate sectors have merged with the statutory education sector. The outcome is that nonprofit organizations and business leaders now play a key role in determining what gets taught in schools and how. Together with policy makers, they write key policy documents, curriculum resources, guidelines for teaching subjects, provide school training for teachers and advisors, contribute to the content of textbooks and examination syllabi, and in some instances shape teacher preparation.

Professor of Education, Elizabeth Heilman observes that global education is mostly advocated by a "white liberal elite" who wish to promote their own global agenda and their Western "global" institutions.[73] Schools that have embraced the global dimension are those that have embraced the values and worldview of this white, liberal elite. Heilman finds that "cosmopolitan global citizenship . . . seeks to shift authority from the local and the national community to a world community that is a loose network of international organizations and subnational political actors not bound within a clear democratic constitutional framework."[74] It is worth asking, who decided that nonprofits and corporations know anything about pedagogy and have the moral right to determine what and how children are taught in schools? For all the rhetoric of values and responsibility used by advocates of global learning, there are big questions to be asked at the level of ethics and democracy when examining the impact of third sector organizations on the progress of education. Not only do the values of these organizations often clash with those of communities, but their agenda for schools are not educational. While intentions are probably well-meaning, business leaders are interested in training children in skills that will be useful in the workplace and nonprofits want children to engage with their political causes and embrace their worldview. This expanded or "global" view of "education" can only distract teachers from the task of educating children about the world.

The flip-side of the growing influence of the corporate and voluntary sectors in American and English schools has been the declining importance of teachers: the very professionals who have been trained to undertake the task in hand. It is the authority of educators that is being undermined in the name of global or international education.

Notes

1 Chandler (2002) p. 21.

2 Ibid. p. 68.

3 Sassens (2002); Kaldor (2005).

4 Kaldor (2005) p. 110.

5 Duffield (2001) p. 53.

6 Ibid. p. 53.

7 Ibid. p. 42.

8 Ibid. p. 42.

9 Kane *et al.* (1990).

10 Ravitch (2010a) p. 199.

11 Ibid. p. 211.

12 CREDO (2009); Ravitch (2010a).

13 Frayn (2010).

14 Ibid.

15 Gates, B., "Prepared Remarks," National Governors Association/ Archive Summit, 2005. Accessed:http://www.nga.org/cda/files/ es05gates.pdf

16 Internationalization Strategic Planning Group, *Global Education Strategic Plan*, Fairleigh Dickinson University. Accessed: http://view. fdu.edu/files/globedstratplan051107.pdf

17 Davis-Salazar, K. and Wells, E., "Citizenship and Sustainability: Towards Global-Reach Curricula," *Anthropology News*, April 2011, p. 13.

18 Ibid.

19 Council for Global Education "Mission Statement." 2009. Accessed: http://www.globaleducation.org/2.htm

20 Asia Society "Why International Knowledge and Skills?" 2011. Accessed: http://asiasociety.org/education-learning/partnership-global-learning/making-case/partnership-global-learning

21 Asia Society "International Education: What are the Goals?" 2007. Accessed: http://www/internationaled.org/goals.htm

22 Schukar (1993).

23 Banks (2002).

24 Gaudelli and Fernekes (2004) pp. 16–26.

25 Librera *et al.* (2005) p. 6.

26 New Jersey Department of Education (2006) *New Jersey Core Curriculum Content Standards for Social Studies*, p. 8

27 New Jersey Department of Education (2006) p. 12.

28 Ibid. p. 15.

29 New Jersey Department of Education (2009) *Revised Core Curriculum Content Standards Posted for Review.* Accessed at: http://www.state.nj.us/education/news/2009/0206cccs.htm

30 Center for International Understanding (2006).

31 Ibid.

32 National Council for Social Studies (2003) *Expectations of Excellence: Curriculum Standards for Social Studies. Accessed:* http://www.socialstudies.org/standards/strands/

33 NCATE (2001) *Standards for Professional Development Schools: Standard IV Diversity and Equity.* Accessed: http://www.ncate.org/LinkClick.aspx?fileticket = P2KEH2wR4Xs%3d&tabid = 107

34 Partnership for 21st Century Skills (2003).

35 Council of Chief State School Officers & the National Governors Association (2010) *Common Core State Standards for English Language Arts & Literacy in History/Social Studies, Science, and Technical Subjects.* Accessed: http://www.corestandards.org/assets/CCSSI_ELA%20Standards.pdf

36 Dillon, S., "Behind Grass-Roots School Advocacy, Bill Gates," *New York Times*, 22 May 2011.

37 Ibid.

38 International Baccalaureate Organization, "United State Country Profile," 2010. Accessed: http://www.ibo.org/iba/countryprofiles/documents/US_CountryProfile.pdf

39 Ibid.

40 Byrd *et al.* (2007).

41 Education News "Protestors Call IB Program un-American. Is it?" 2010. Accessed at: http://www.educationnews.org/ednews_today/91338.html

42 Ibid.

43 Hicks (2003).

44 Critchley and Unwin (2008) p. 4.

45 Advisory Group on Citizenship (1998).

46 Marshall (2005).

47 Oxfam (1997).

48 Bourn and Hunt (2011) p. 35.

49 Ibid. p. 35.

50 Department for Education and Skills/Department for International Development (2005) p. 2.

51 Central Bureau/Development Education Association (2000).

52 Development Education Association, *Citizenship Education: The Global Dimension*, 2001. Accessed: http://www.globaldimension.org.uk/resourcesearch/details.aspx?id = 959

53 Development Education Association, *Geography: The Global Dimension: Key Stage 3*, 2004.

54 Department for International Development, "Partnership Programme Arrangements," 2010. Accessed: www.dfid.gov

55 Department for International Development, "Global Schools Partnerships," 2011. Accessed: http://www.dfid.gov.uk/get-involved/for-schools/global-school-partnerships/

56 Critchley and Unwin (2008) p. 9.

57 Humanities Education Centre. Accessed: http://www.globalfootprints.org/

58 Bourn and Hunt (2011).

59 Baughen *et al.* (2006).

60 Local4global, "London and the South East Regions," Accessed: http://www.local4global.org.uk/

61   Center for Global Perspectives, "About the University," Bournemouth University. Accessed: http://www.bournemouth.ac.uk/about/the_global_dimension/centre_for_global_perspectives/centre_for_global_perspectives.html

62   Gallagher, S. and O'Hara, G., *Local and Global Citizenship for CCEA GCSE – Learning for Life and Work*. Hodder Education, 2004.

63   Algarra, B., *Key Stage 3 Workbook: Media and the Global Dimension*. Philip Allen, 2007.

64   Burtenshaw, D., *A2 Geography Edexcel (B) Unit 4: Global Challenge (Population and the Economy)*. Philip Allen, 2000.

65   Bunnell (2008).

66   International Baccalaureate Schools and Colleges Association, 2011. Accessed: http://www.ibsca.org.uk/

67   Department for Education and Skills (2004) p. 1.

68   Ibid. p. 3.

69   Bourn and Hunt (2011) p. 5.

70   Ibid. p. 15.

71   Ibid. p. 34.

72   Department for Education (2010) p. 10.

73   Heilman (2009) p. 32.

74   Ibid. p. 33.

3

Global knowledge

This chapter will examine the case for global knowledge: what it is, why it is deemed to be necessary, how it is taught, how it is different from subject-based knowledge, and will it lead to better educated and better prepared young people?

On both sides of the Atlantic, there has been growing skepticism about whether the subject-based curriculum meets the needs of today's children. It is suggested that, while the subject-based curriculum was created for integrating children into bounded national democracies, national cultures, and national economies, today's global world is characterized by rapid change and fluidity, where knowledge and skills need to be continually updated.[1] Therefore, young people need to learn to be flexible, adaptable, willing to migrate, and work with people of different culture. They need to be able to update their knowledge and skills on a regular basis to keep up with new information and technological change. In the opinion of Asia Society Director Michael Levine, "young people who understand the dynamics of global economic and intercultural relations will have a distinct advantage in securing good jobs," arising from "knowledge of world history, languages, global health and international affairs."[2] Such an approach typically places education directly in service of the economy.

The case for global knowledge is made by advocates of global citizenship as well as those in the businesses world. The academic curriculum is regarded by some as too abstract and detached from the lives of children and excludes non-Western, nonelite perspectives. In contrast, "Global education has long recognized that any understanding of the contemporary world needs to be based on participatory and experiential ways of learning. It needs to involve both head and heart (the cognitive and affective) and the personal and political (values clarification and political literacy)."[3] With global education the emphasis is often on enquiry and participation, constructing your own knowledge, rather than mastery of knowledge developed by experts (theoretical knowledge). Global knowledge is presented as future-orientated, issue-based, inclusive, child-centered, tolerant of other cultures, multilingual, integrative, and sensitive to different perspectives. Here it is worth reviewing these claims, and asking whether they are as unequivocally positive as they sound.

Future-orientated

While subject disciplines are concerned with educating children about the past and the present (accumulated knowledge), it is argued that global education aims to prepare them for the future. For some people, subject-knowledge is seen as a "hangover" from a Victorian age.[4] Subject knowledge is disliked by many on the Left because of its association with the rule of national elites, discussed further below. While schooling in the US and England has historically served multiple economic, social, political, and welfare functions, overall, schools sought to integrate children into the society by passing on the society's intellectual and cultural traditions.[5] This does not make teachers ignorant of change, nor does it deprive children of the opportunity to shape an alternative future. On the contrary, only when young people are equipped with the insights of previous generations are they well-placed to improve society. We suggest that a key reason why global education has cultural purchase in society today is because of disenchantment with the intellectual and cultural legacy of nations.

In place of bounded disciplines, global knowledge can be almost any knowledge: whatever it is that society determines children need to grow up in the twenty-first century. In place of packaging knowledge into discrete subjects, the global approach encourages teachers to pursue cross-curricula themes, issues, key concepts, or skills, which are presented as more pertinent to the needs of pupils.

In order to develop global knowledge, pupils are asked to think about how society could do things differently to build an alternative future, instead of carrying on in the same way. For example, in a chapter about teaching geography for a sustainable future, Alun Morgan highlights the importance of sustainability (a key theme of global education) as a concept when planning for the future:

Sustainable development is concerned with improving the quality of people's lives, both their economic security and their social well being, without destroying the systems on which their future generations depend. Sustainability is the main outcome. It is future orientated."[6]

Morgan includes a number of possible activities to encourage children to think about sustainable and unsustainable futures. Strategy 1: Probable and Preferable Futures (Box 3.1) is one of these activities, in which pupils draw timelines with different branches for alternative paths. After the activity is completed, children are

---

BOX 3.1   ENVISIONING THE FUTURE[7]

Strategy 1: Probable and preferable futures

A very simple device to help students to think about their own images of the future is the 'probable/preferable futures timeline'. Students are asked to consider an issue. It may be one that relates to them personally (e.g. their personal ambition) or to people collectively (i.e. the community), and can operate over any spatial scale from the local (e.g. employment, traffic issues) to the global (e.g. climate change). They then draw a single time-line outlining crucial events relating to the issue up to the present, their time-line then forks into two branches. The probable (usually the lower limb) is labeled with the likely events that would occur, given the existing trajectory. The preferable (upper limb) is labeled with the events that the student(s) would like to see happen.

Reproduced from 'Teaching Geography for a Sustainable Future' by Alun Morgan with permission from the Geographical Association.

asked to discuss the different decisions and actions that could lead society down each branch. "A major educational justification is that futures education is more relevant to the needs of young people and consequently is likely to be more engaging, thereby raising achievement through enhanced motivation," asserts Morgan.[8]

Morgan's comments imply discomfort with teaching about the past; that somehow learning about our history, culture, and how we came to arrive at today's world will not be motivating for children. It seems that the turn toward about the future is better understood as a product of the uncertainty its advocates hold toward society's accumulated wisdom, rather than a response to some different needs of the present generation.

Issues-based

Global issues are deemed to be transnational problems, or challenges the world faces at the beginning of the twenty-first century. Commonly addressed global issues in many schools include poverty and malnutrition, environmental and ecological problems (especially global warming), equity, peace and conflict resolution, health, human rights, social justice, population growth, sustainable development, trade, and technological change. The list of global issues reflects the work of development and other nonprofit groups, and also the United Nations (for example, see the UN Millennium Development Goals[9]). As we saw in the previous chapter, many of these groups have published teaching materials on global issues for schools. Here, we will look at a lesson activity simulating fair trade, produced by the Reading International Solidarity Centre (RISC), which serves an area of Berkshire, England.

The lesson "Growing Bananas" (Box 3.2), designed for Key Stage 2–3 (ages: 7–14 years), introduces pupils to agricultural production and trade. In this activity, children "grow" (i.e. draw) bananas to sell to the teacher in exchange for fictional dollars, but each year experience either some boon to their production or adversity that leads to additional expenses. Here, pupils learn about some of the challenges a banana farmer might experience in trying to manage their business. Such activities are not uncommon in social studies or geography classes, although often more realistic and sophisticated than this example. However, RISC's "Growing Bananas" activity

BOX 3.2 GROWING BANANAS ACTIVITY[10]

- *Organize students into groups of 4 or 5.*
- *Each group of students represents a family growing bananas in the Windward Islands.*
- *The simulation should run for at least 3 rounds, each round representing a year of banana growing.*
- *At the start, each group should allocate a member to complete their 'balance sheet'.*

During each round:

- *The groups should use scrap paper to 'grow' bananas, by drawing, coloring and cutting them out.*
- *Offer each group an event card from a selection of upturned chance cards (see below). They should respond to the information on their card by entering it on their balance sheet.*
- *Once each group has an event card, announce that it is time to trade. Each group should deliver their completed bananas to the teacher/facilitator, along with their chance card. Tell each group how much they have earned (roughly $100 works best). They must then add or subtract according to the instructions on their change card. Finally each group decides how to allocate their money.*

Sample Event/Chance Cards

Your roof is leaking badly, and you have to fix it. One person can't grow bananas this round.	*Your children need to start secondary school. It will cost you $50 each year.*
Your son is ill. You need to spend $10 on medicine this year.	*Pests have attacked your banana trees. You'll receive half price for your lower quality crop.*
You've produced a bumper crop this year- you make an extra $20!	*A Fairtrade company have offered to buy your entire crop—as long as you stop using pesticides. This year you'll receive 50% more for your crop.*

(Continued)

UK consumers are buying more
of your Fairtrade bananas—you
can sell another 25% of your crop
through Fairtrade and receive an
extra 10% each year.

With Fairtrade, you can no longer
use weed killers. One person must
stop growing bananas to weed
between the trees.

Reproduced from Growing Bananas: A Simulation about Fair
Trade for KS2-3 (2005) with permission from Reading International Solidarity Centre.

was designed to promote the idea of fair trade and encourage
children to "empathize with Caribbean banana growers": developing an understanding of the challenges of agricultural production
in small, underdeveloped islands is not included as an aim of the
activity.[11] With fair-trade products, the farmer usually receives an
incrementally larger share of the commodity's sale price, but has
to agree to some restrictions on production such as not using pesti-
cides. At the end of the activity, teachers are encouraged to debrief
the class summarizing "the importance of Fairtrade," "the use of the
Fairtrade Mark," and also "our impact as consumers."[12]

The purpose of this teaching resource (which was supported by
AgroFair, Banana Link, and the Fairtrade Foundation) is clearly to
encourage children to support the idea of fair trade and buy fairtrade products. This is achieved through a simplistic presentation
of trade and how fair trade can give farmers slightly more of the
proceeds. This seems to be more of a marketing exercise than an
educational endeavor; it does not lead pupils to an understanding
of the challenges faced by small farmers in less developed countries,
but instead aims to engage children emotionally in a political
cause.

The term "global issues" is problematic because it tends to
ignore the local and cultural context in which issues or problems
arise. A "global" problem is one that has been removed from its
geographical and political context, without due consideration to
local economic, historical, cultural, or environmental factors. For
example, a Peruvian farmer will view deforestation in an entirely
different way than someone in New York City or London. Instead

of educating children about the cultural and economic contexts which lead people to think and act as they do, the global approach tends to assume that problems are the same the world over. In other words, it is assumed that everybody does—or should—look at these issues in the same way as Western globalists.

The global approach also presents issues as the responsibility of children, as exemplified by the Fairtrade example cited above. This is why teaching materials and global education documents emphasize pupil *awareness* and *engagement* with the issue, often resulting in some kind of action. "Students will develop a sense of efficacy and civic responsibility by identifying specific ways that they can make some contribution to the resolution of a global issue or challenge," suggest the authors of Wisconsin's *Planning Curriculum in International Education*.[13] In the national curriculum for England, children at key stage two (ages: 7–11 years) are expected to "develop their sense of social justice and moral responsibility and begin to understand that their own choices can affect global issues, as well as local ones."[14] At the level of secondary education, it is expected that children "realize the importance of taking action and how this can improve the world for future generations," and "challenge cases of discrimination and justice."[15]

Children of all ages are expected to learn about global issues and engage in their resolution. "Elementary students are perfectly capable of comprehending, analyzing, and proposing solutions to global problems," suggests the Wisconsin Department of Public Instruction.[16] Yet while a skilled teacher is able to present that which is complex in simple terms, this does not mean that children will understand problems in their complexity. In another RISC activity, taken from *Growing up Global: Early Years Global Education Handbook*, children are given unequal amounts of raisins as an introduction to the idea of fair and unfair trade.[17] Yet, this activity is quite clearly not about fair trade at all—just unfairness. It is also more than a little strange to attempt to engage infants in a discussion of international trade before they have learned to read.

Indeed, many so-called global issues are considered highly complex by academics and scientists: the causes of poverty, global warming, what is meant by social justice, and so forth. This does not mean that children should not study the issues and probable causes; they certainly should, and there are examples of strong issue-based approaches, such as Brown's Choices Program.[18] But in order to engage seriously in a discussion of solutions to problems, "students must understand the problem to be solved, have the necessary information for solving it, and know solutions to similar problems."[19] This means that children will need to have learned considerable background knowledge both in the relevant subject areas (environmental science, ecology, biology, weather and climate, market economics, political science, sociology, cultural systems, demography, or history) and the specific geographical locations, as well as having at least a rudimentary knowledge of the functioning of political systems and government. Alternatively, a creative teacher might use one of these problems as a lead into in-depth subject knowledge; for example, the division of Sudan as a lead into the cultural and political geography of Africa. But when issues are discussed without, or instead of, the knowledge needed to comprehend them, a serious problem arises. This is why detailed study of such issues will have more success in the latter years of schooling: and then, only if students are equipped with enough knowledge in the first place. As a recent government inspection report on the state of geography teaching in English secondary schools remarked:

> Although pupils were often encouraged well to consider complex global issues such as migration and inequalities of wealth, their understanding was frequently unsatisfactory. This was because the learning was not set sufficiently within the context of real and recognizable places, so their understanding did not develop beyond an awareness that such issues existed.[20]

In the eyes of global educators, learning about global issues has more to do with emotionally engaging children in political causes identified by nonprofit groups and activists than it does with understanding the complexities of life in different parts of the world. But to be *aware* and *engaged* with a global issue doesn't necessarily demand much in the way of knowledge and understanding. Furthermore, telling children that they have a responsibility for global issues around the world raises some important moral questions about the nature of global education, as does the Western bias implicit in global issues. These will be discussed in more detail in the chapter "Global Ethics."

Including the voices
of excluded others

The modernizing rhetoric of global education helps to explain its appeal, especially at a time when our relationship to the past has become fraught. Arguably, it is this desire to escape the past, and specifically the historical record of nation states (colonialism, elitism, world war), which is driving the rejection of expert knowledge by those seeking a global or international approach to education. Because disciplinary knowledge and school subjects were developed by national elites, frequently in the service of nations, they are viewed by some as integral to the rule of nation states and the disciplining of citizens. As Johan Muller explains, some constructivist teachers view the academic curriculum as a Eurocentric "tool of modernity" with "imperialistic roots" and instead seek a "pedagogical project aimed at incorporating examples from the life-world of learners from a variety of race, gender, class and cultural backgrounds."[21] Thus, a relativist approach to knowledge is adopted that celebrates all knowledge as equally valid.

For instance Jaya Graves, the coordinator of Southern Voices, campaigns for the need to include non-Western voices in the curriculum. Southern Voices is a small nonprofit organization in Manchester, England, committed to "presenting views, perspectives and voices of people from Southern or 'developing' countries."[22] Similarly, Camicia and Saavedra of Utah State University advocate for a new social studies curriculum that is not based upon "Eurocentric, androcentric and United State-centric notions of citizenship," which they suggest devalues the voices of children; instead, they would like to see a transnational concept of citizenship which privileges "the perspectives of our racial, ethnic, poor, and transnational students."[23] For this reason, textbooks and other teaching materials frequently include sections or boxes describing life or events from the perspective of others (although rarely include different perspectives on global issues).

Recognizing the perspectives of others is an important part of learning because it teaches one to abstract from personal experience. However, learning about different people's experiences or perspectives is not the same thing as developing an understanding of theoretical knowledge. And, when the two are equated, theoretical knowledge is devalued and pupils may be deprived of the insights of subject disciplines.

For an example of a curriculum constructed around the principle of inclusion, and its antiintellectual consequences, we need to look no further than the English National Curriculum. English teacher Michele Ledda describes how the content of the English curriculum has been determined not by the esthetic quality of literature, but instead using an "equal opportunities" method. He writes:

> Today's canon is mainly determined by behind-the-scenes decisions made by examination boards through complication consultation processes which have very little to do with the quality of the works to be studied and more with a preoccupation to include every possible religion, ethnicity, or culture and to make sure that there is a gender balance.[24]

Ledda cites the example of the way poems are selected for the *Assessment and Qualifications Alliance (AQA) Anthology* for General Certificate in Secondary Education (GCSE) courses in English and English Literature. The first of the two sections consists of 16 poems from different cultures including India (4), Pakistan (1), the Caribbean (5), Africa (3), Scotland (1), and the US (2). Nine of the poems were written by men and seven by women. Pupils must study eight of these poems, thus covering a range of cultures and gender. In the second section, 48 poems were mostly written by four contemporary British poets (two men and two women). Candidates select four of these poems to write about, which must include one by a woman and one by a man. Ledda objects to the focus on contemporary poets, such as Carol Ann Duffy, who are perceived to be more "relevant" to young people because they write about topics children can identify with, such as disaffected learners or urban life. Meanwhile, "The whole tradition of English poetry from its origins to 1914 is represented by 16 poems."[25]

Although not specified, it appears that the Assessment and Qualification Alliance and other examination boards are making decisions about which literary works pupils should study based upon the author's gender, where they are from, and whether or not they write about topics of direct relevance to children, instead of their literary value. But how are pupils going to learn how to recognize and write imaginatively and creatively if they are not exposed to literature of the highest order? The problem with the value of inclusion is that it discourages evaluation of literary merit, notes Ledda. "Such a value makes a mockery of all the values included, the condition for inclusion being that no one particular point of view is taken entirely seriously."[26] A curriculum constructed in the name of inclusion can only achieve that which it set out to: including different perspectives. Unless pupils are encouraged to make judgments about what makes literature better or worse they will never learn the difference. And when adults are refusing to make these judgments themselves in devising the curriculum, it is a sure sign that they have aims for the curriculum which are straying from education. Instead of cultivating an appreciation of literature, language, or another subject, curricula built around the idea of inclusion are primarily concerned to instill in children politically correct notions of inclusion and nonjudgmentalism.

Child-centered

When theoretical knowledge is placed on par with personal experiences, anybody is deemed capable of developing "knowledge," even children. From here it is easy to see why global education emphasizes child-centeredness and enquiry learning over theoretical knowledge acquisition.[27] With enquiry learning, pupils are encouraged to pose their own questions, devise a research strategy, and find information to help them answer questions. Thus, it is argued, they are constructing knowledge for themselves, rather than just receiving knowledge generated by experts.

The enquiry methodology of teaching can be creative and stimulating for pupils when employed effectively by a skilled practitioner. As any good teacher knows, understanding is deeper and more lasting when pupils reach conclusions by themselves. While there are times when a teacher has to lecture or give children answers, teachers will frequently ask probing questions or provide challenging material that disrupts a simplistic level of understanding in order to view phenomena in greater complexity. This is done with a view to helping pupils to access theoretical knowledge. In contrast, the priority given to enquiry learning by global educators has more to do with the displacement of, and distrust for, expert-led subject knowledge than it does with exploratory teaching methods.

For example, in an article discussing the potential contribution of a global approach to the enhancement of gender equality, Harriet Marshall and Madeleine Arnot show how such critical pedagogy differs from the academic curriculum:

> Critical pedagogues in developed nations aim to create dialogue engagement and ownership amongst those disadvantaged by the social biases and negative representations found in school texts, teaching materials and teaching strategies. The aim of much critical pedagogy is to make clear to students that the curriculum is a site of meaning making and that the social construction of knowledge opens up possibilities of including their knowledge. Increasingly, the voices and lived experiences of male and female youth have been drawn into the curriculum arena challenging dominant 'expert' and hierarchical organized knowledge forms.[28]

The authors here are effectively saying there is nothing special about "expert and hierarchical organized forms of knowledge," these are just one version of socially constructed knowledge to which children should add their own. While it is true that all knowledge is socially constructed, this relativistic approach to knowledge fails to distinguish between knowledge as organized concepts and ideas developed by educated people over thousands of years and the limited life experiences of school children. The "voices and lived experiences" of youth may be of interest to them but they will not help children to understand social and natural phenomena in a way that subject expertise can. As Peter Gardenfors explains, the "orthodox constructivist viewpoint demands too much of the students: they are supposed to discover the patterns that took scientists and professors centuries to uncover."[29] The outcome of the child-centered approach is that they may feel good about their discoveries, but they will be left without the knowledge and insights of generations of adults.

Cultural tolerance

Multiculturalism has been an important theme of American education for more than three decades and at least two decades in

England. It has some common aims with global education, including teaching about pluralism rather than taking a monocultural approach, a focus on cultural identity, and a celebration of cultural diversity. Where it differs is that global education takes culture out of the national context to explore different cultures from around the world and their unique histories. Instead of being about "us," it is about "us and the Other."[30] In fact, the global approach elevates the values of liberal elites and global progressives over those of national and local cultures. In the end, it has very little to do with "us."

What do children need to learn about global cultures? According to Wisconsin's *Planning Curriculum in International Education*, students should:

- Develop a broad understanding of major geographic and cultural areas of the world.
- Understand that there are universals connecting all cultures.
- Understand that members of different cultures view the world in different ways.
- Understand that individuals may identify with more than one culture and thus have multiple loyalties.
- Appropriately tolerate cultural diversity.
- Seek to meet and communicate with people from other cultures.
- Demonstrate an appreciation of universal human rights.
- Move outside the classroom to participate in cultural, arts, and folk arts activities in authentic settings. [31]

Here, we have a mixture of cultural knowledge, values, skills, and activities. There are many ways that schools have been advised to approach the teaching of world cultures. Schools are told that they can draw upon the experiences and knowledge of pupils who come from different cultural backgrounds. Children can share their different cultural experiences through dress, festivals, holidays, food, stories, and belief systems. Schools can also invite guest speakers, who might be someone living in the community, to visit the school to talk about their cultural background.

In recent years, more schools have found partner schools in other countries to communicate with. In England, the Department for

International Development created the Global School Partnerships scheme to help schools find an international partner. "School partnerships helps students understand the world beyond their shores – through accessing the experiences of other children who are living in different cultures and traditions," suggests the report *The World Classroom: Developing Global Partnerships in Education.*[32] Partner schools write letters to each other, hold discussions on the Internet, and sometimes work together on joint projects. Another way that schools are encouraged to provide children with experiences of other cultures is through travel abroad and international student/ teacher exchange programs. All of these can provide valuable experience and insight into other cultures, but this is only part of the reason for the cultural focus of global learning. From the above planning guide, we can see how teaching about culture is tied to the promotion of tolerance. This aim has changed little over time for advocates of international education. Indeed, many teachers and parents support the value of tolerance in education.

However, what has changed is the meaning of tolerance in contemporary Anglo-American culture. In the seventeenth century, John Stuart Mill and John Locke promoted the social value of tolerance as freedom of consciousness from the intervention of the state.[33] For these classical thinkers, tolerating different opinions encouraged open debate and political engagement, ideas essential to modern democracies. In contrast, tolerance promoted by liberal elites and global progressives today is "often represented as a form of nonjudgmental acceptance of other people's beliefs."[34] Such an approach dissuades intellectual and moral engagement, suggests sociologist Frank Furedi. The ethic of tolerance is discussed further in Chapter 5. Here, we note its growing significance in the curriculum and how the nonjudgmental approach toward tolerance inhibits learning academic knowledge.

Some subject disciplines have also reinvented themselves as a medium for teaching politically correct tolerance. Geography naturally lends itself to a study of human diversity across the Earth's surface, and the focus on the global dimension in the curriculum, as well as tolerance, has undoubtedly improved the standing of geography in many American and English schools. In world geography classes, pupils learn about how countries and cultures differ from region to region.

There has also been a shift in focus from teaching about the history of Europe and America to world history. In place of a focus on the historical rise of the West, many schools now include a brief history of China, India, Africa, South America, and Central America. One report found that "the percentage of American students taking world history and world geography in high school has risen faster than enrolment in any other social studies classes over the past 15 years."[35] Data from the 2005 National Assessment for Academic Progress revealed that 77 per cent of high school graduates had taken a world history class and 31 per cent had taken world geography (up from 21 per cent in 1990). In response to the increased demand for world geography and world history, the College Board created the Advanced Placement (AP) Human Geography course in 2001, which was followed a year later by AP World History (Advanced Placement classes are designed to be equivalent to an introductory class at college or university).

Expanding history and geography beyond the people and regions of one's own country broadens children's minds and aids their understanding of these subjects. I have observed Advanced Placement world history classes in which motivated children were conducting detailed research into the lives of historical figures in non-Western regions. Similarly, in world geography classes, pupils study the lives of people in settings that are completely different to their own. If this was all there was to these changes, this could be a positive development. Unfortunately, too often the motivation for teaching world history and world geography has more to do with instilling a relativistic, nonjudgmental disposition which discourages children from the critical engagement with both subject content and morality. Cultural relativism also fails to teach children about their own culture. Learning about one's own culture is important not because children should embrace their own culture and national perspective in an uncritical way, as those on the Right might have it. Rather, when children are grounded in their own culture it gives them a sense of belonging to a wider community and also a basis from which to draw comparisons with other cultures and perspectives.

Social studies teacher Jonathan Burack found AP World History lacking in clear unifying principles to select the facts, nations, and trends to be covered. Instead of telling history as an unfolding narrative to explain the evolution of human civilization, AP World History covers the themes of: global interaction, change and continuity, technology, social structure, diversity, and gender. Burack found that the majority of the course (at least 70 per cent) emphasizes non-Western societies and downplays the role of the West.[36] "Without solid historical content and a strong grounding in their own Western cultural heritage, students will not be able to grasp fully how other cultures differ," retorts Burack.[37]

Also reduced to a bit-part role are nation states and politics. Burack suggested that AP World History instead was laden with a "global ideology" of "multicultural celebration, cultural relativism, and transnational progressivism."[38] Here, diversity of cultural history seems to have been included for the sake of promoting the value of diversity itself, rather than because it aided an exploration of culture or history in different societies. Burack notes that the multicultural approach lacked a systematic concept of culture through which societies could be compared:

> Such a concept would define and explain the linkages among family structure, kinship groupings, language, technology, religion, art, and ethical norms and laws. Far more common, however, is a seemingly random selection of disparate elements that are often superficial or exotic: clothing styles, food, holidays, religious observances, leisure activities, rituals, and other customs.[39]

Burack found this approach also true with world history textbooks. While cultural elements such as fabrics, rituals, or food were included, there was no attempt to link these to an understanding of the social beliefs and structures that gave rise to them. In other words, this is an a-cultural approach whose "primary purpose appears to be to get students to recognize the achievements of the various African peoples mentioned."[40] Here, the objective is one of validating other cultures in the minds of American pupils, even though the course fails to explore both the meaning of culture and its historical development in different regions.

The sad case of the English History National Curriculum tells a similar story. Head Teacher and educational advisor Chris McGovern explains how, from the 1980s, history as a coherent body of knowledge was gradually replaced with a subject focused on "skills" and "perspectives." He describes how the New History was all about "value relativism" because history was now being presented as a "matter of opinion."[41] This led to a focus on non-European history and the elevation of perspectives over knowledge:

> The National Curriculum document states that children must be taught history through four 'diversity' perspectives – 'the social, cultural, religious, and ethnic diversity of the societies studied'. In addition, perspectives on 'experiences', on 'ideas', on 'beliefs', and on 'attitudes' relating to each of men, women and children, must be taught . . . . This amounts to another 12 perspectives. The focus on perspectives is spelt out explicitly in the statement requiring that history be taught 'from a variety of perspectives including political, religious, social, cultural, aesthetic, economic, technological and scientific', a further eight perspectives.[42]

In all, McGovern counted twenty-four perspectives being promoted in the History National Curriculum. Identifying the true perspective of others is a useful mechanism for understanding the social, cultural, and political context which leads people to think and act as they do. To understand a perspective genuinely, one must scrutinize the ideas being put forth so that one can make intellectual and moral judgments about them. However, the global approach of tolerating perspectives has the effect of dissuading pupils from this engagement, and the understanding and ethical deliberation that would follow.

In the History National Curriculum, McGovern describes how history becomes "all a matter of opinion."[43] Here, history has been relegated from an intellectual pursuit that informs us about our past and how different people have shaped the world in their images. Instead of advancing the historical knowledge and understanding of children, the New History curriculum only requires an *awareness* of different opinions.

Multilingual

Perhaps more so than other subjects, the place of world languages in American and English schools reveals the gap between the innovative rhetoric of global education and the reality of declining knowledge about the world, in this case languages. Numerous school policy documents produced in the past decade highlight the importance of learning at least one foreign language in today's "global world." For example, the UK government's key initiative *Languages for All: Languages for Life: A Strategy for England* asserted, "In the knowledge society of the 21st century, language competence and intercultural understanding are not optional extras, they are an essential part of being a citizen."[44] If governments and schools were really committed to the teaching of foreign languages we would see a concerted effort to dramatically expand the training of teachers to teach different languages and more schools offering an indepth study of foreign languages, literature, and culture, such that all children understand and are fluent in more than one language. Unfortunately, data from schools suggest otherwise.

Although there have been initiatives in both the US and England to expand the teaching of foreign languages, they have been somewhat half-hearted, often sending mixed messages. For instance, the National Strategy for Languages in England claimed that it would "transform our country's capability in languages." The strategy included offering foreign languages to pupils in primary schools, a new credit system for language skills, increased opportunities for adults in higher education and workplaces, and new training opportunities for teaching a foreign language. The strategy document rightly highlights the infrequency of foreign language teaching at elementary level as a problem, as well as the dearth of primary teachers trained to teach them. The National Strategy has at least made an impact on foreign language offerings in primary education. In 2008, 92 per cent of primary schools were teaching a foreign language and 69 per cent were offering this throughout Years 3–6 (ages: 7–11).[45] This is approximately double the number of schools teaching foreign languages since the launch of the National Strategy in 2002.

Taken at face value, this is a significant progress. However, the National Strategy only stipulates that schools must offer children an *entitlement* to foreign languages rather than requiring them to study it. Surely, if foreign languages are of educational value, shouldn't all pupils study them? Unfortunately, the National Foundation for Education Research report does not include data showing how many children are actually taking up their entitlement.

The failure to require all children to study a foreign language is a particular problem at secondary school level. While in the majority of schools pupils must take a second language between the ages of 11 and 14, the National Strategy recommended that they remain optional (an "entitlement") from this juncture. Thus, in most state schools (70 per cent) the study of a foreign language is no longer compulsory after Year 9 (age: 14), a requirement that was axed by the New Labour government in 2004.[46] The decline of participation in foreign languages postfourteen has been precipitous over recent years: for Year 10 (ages: 14–15) declining from 48 per cent in 2005 to 40 per cent in 2009 and for Year 11 (age 15–16) from 53 per cent (2005) to 43 per cent (2009).[47] One of the reasons for this decline is that both pupils and adults "perceive languages as a hard, academic subject," suggests the National Center for Languages/Association for Language Learning report.[48] Therefore, while children might be starting a foreign language earlier in the English state school system, most are also giving it up earlier because some adults are giving them the message that it is not important to go on studying languages.

In the private sector, things are different. There is both a richer offering of foreign languages and participation rates are higher. In 82 per cent of private schools the study of a foreign language is compulsory up to age sixteen.[49] The report concludes: "There is a conspicuous gap in access to language learning between pupils in the state and independent sectors."[50]

In the US, the story is similar. Again, the rhetoric speaks to the importance, if not the necessity, of learning a second language for life in multicultural communities and work in a global market. Yet, survey data from the Center for Applied Linguistics show that instruction in most foreign languages has declined over the past decade, with the exception of Chinese (which was offered in just 1 per cent of middle and high schools in 1998 but rose to 4 per cent in 2008).[51] While there were tiny increases in the number of schools offering Italian and Hebrew, and the number offering Spanish remained unchanged, Greek, Russian, Japanese, Latin, German, and French all experienced declines (between 0.3 and 18 per cent) in the number of schools offering these languages.

The teaching of Standard Chinese (Mandarin) has been helped by increasing business ties between the US and China, just as the teaching of Japanese increased in the 1980s. The Chinese government for one is sending teachers from China to teach in American schools and in other countries, and often paying their salaries. There is also a joint program by the College Board and Hanban, a language council affiliated with the Chinese Education Ministry, which has brought hundreds of American teachers and superintendents to China to visit schools. The survey data suggest that Chinese is now being taught in approximately 1,600 American public and private schools, up from 300 a decade ago.[52] Spanish continues to be the most taught foreign language, being offered in 88 per cent of elementary schools and 93 per cent of middle and high schools.

The problems with foreign language teaching do not stop with its lack of quantitative growth. More perceptive observers will have noted a subtle but very important shift in the way that languages are discussed, in policy circles at least. Rarely do advocates talk about a foreign language as a subject to be mastered, but rather view it as a skill to be acquired. Here, the emphasis upon *doing* rather than *knowing* implies a superficial approach to language. Abstract and theoretical knowledge are reduced to the practical, immediate, and relevant. This change has happened over the past two decades as policy makers and educators have sought to justify the teaching of foreign languages through their utility in the global marketplace, and more recently as an ethical responsibility of global citizens. The outcome has been reduced expectations for learning a language. As Shirley Lawes reports, "the emphasis on the functional use of language in practical situations paved the way for an emptying out of any serious linguistic or cultural content in favor of what was to become little more than a survival toolkit for a holiday abroad."[53] Again, we can see that the rhetoric and the reality do not add up. As Lawes points out, while schools are frequently offering pupils no more than some basic linguistic understanding, "mastery of a foreign language is a lifetime pursuit."[54] This means that while many pupils are exposed to a second language, what they leave schools with is well below the level required in the workplace to communicate effectively in another language. This is not to suggest that the teaching of foreign languages in either English or American state school was of a high standard in the past, but at least there was an expectation that learning another language was something that all children needed as part of their education and that this took years of study. In England at least, it is the private sector who are now contributing the majority of foreign language students to universities.

Global connections

A common theme found in American and English curricula today is that of global connections or international interdependence. Wisconsin's *Planning Curriculum in International Education* includes *global connections* alongside *global cultures* and *global challenges* as the three strands of international education. Its rationale for learning about global connections states:

> A focus on global connections helps students see the ways their daily lives are affected by change and interdependence. They begin to see how their lives are affected by complex systems involving environmental issues, political policies, demographic shifts, international trade and diverse ideologies and religions.[55]

The planning guide includes examples of how to teach about global connections and simultaneously cover Wisconsin's Academic Standards. Some examples of these lesson activities are provided in Box 3.3.

These examples illustrate how global education includes a mixture of the insightful (product and production webs), the mundane (unequal handfuls of popcorn), and the moralistic (consumer behavior). Intellectually, there is much to be learned about the connections between local, regional, national, and international scales. This applies to economics, history, culture, language, technology, politics, and the natural environment. Such connections are not new, although changing political circumstances (end of the Cold War) and technological advancement (e.g. the Internet) have facilitated the extent of international cooperation and exchange. The interconnected nature of our world was not lost to the teaching of subjects in the past.

What is unique about the global approach is the way in which phenomena and events in the world are presented as connected to,

BOX 3.3   INTERNATIONAL EDUCATION CONNECTIONS TO WISCONSIN'S MODEL STANDARDS[56]

a) Environmental Education: Global Connections Activities

Population density: *Divide popcorn among children, who are arranged in groups according to population. When some children get much and others get less, introduce concepts of global geography, continents, and population. See Zero Population Growth for curriculum materials and statistics. (elementary level)*

Urbanization and megacities: *Explain how motor vehicle use contributes to air pollution, global warming, and ozone depletion. Identify actions that individuals can take to reduce the environmental impact of motor vehicles. See World Resources Institute activity "Car Trouble". (high school)*

b) Family and Consumer Education: Global Connections Activities

Global marketplace: *Create and discuss projects to understand how consumer behavior constitutes voting in the global marketplace. Consumer Economics: A Teacher's Guide, modules 1.10-1.12.*

Choices for the 21st Century Education Project, Voting in the Global Marketplace curriculum unit. (middle or high school)

c) Marketing Education: Global Connections Activities

Global markets: *Choose a specific product. Make a web map showing as many interactions as possible, both negative and positive, that stretch across at least four countries. Include product design, hiring, managing workers, labor policies, production, waste productions, marketing, purchasing, and using, recycling, and disposing of the product. (middle or high school)*

(Continued)

> **Wisconsin's connections to global markets:** *Research ways in which local companies are connected by imports, exports, needs, and services to countries abroad. (upper elementary/ middle/high school)*
>
> Reprinted from *Planning Curriculum in International Education* (2002) with permission from the Wisconsin Department of Public Instruction, 125 S. Webster Street, Madison, WI 53703.

and thus the responsibility of, children. Geographer David Hicks makes the case that global education "involves both head and heart":

> By taking a systems view of the world we are reminded that everything is literally connected to everything else. It is thus not enough to do a project simply on growing bananas and where they come from, whatever geographical insights this may develop . . . . To explore the living condition for banana growers, to look at what they earn, the costs of shipping, the cut the retailer takes, and the price we pay for bananas in the shop, begins to expose webs of interconnection that may also relate to issues of inequality and dependency . . . . Understanding these connections highlights the role we play in different systems, we are not separate . . . but inextricably bound together, and with this should come some sense of shared responsibility for the 'other'.[57]

For its advocates, "global connections" have replaced the nation as a framework for understanding the child's place in the world. For those who view the national framework as discredited, the global approach solves "the problem of meaning."[58] This is why global connections aim to show children how their lives are related to global processes and issues, even if such connections are often tenuous and imperceptible. In theory, it gives some sort of meaning to children's values and actions. However, changing one's consumption habits or recycling waste are extremely limited ways to express one's human potential. This global ethical framework is explored further in Chapter 5.

Conclusion: A flight from knowledge

With global education, theoretical knowledge is undermined because it has been placed on par with people's stories or personal experiences. This "personalized knowledge" is that which is of direct relevance to children's immediate lives: identity, employability, feelings of self-worth. "There is no *knowledge* for voices discourses, only the power of some groups to assert that their experiences should count as knowledge," writes Michael Young.[59] But without subject knowledge there is no education. Knowledge of immediate relevance does not allow one to see beyond personal circumstances and *restricts* the possibility of considering alternative futures.

Everyday knowledge does have its place in schools, but without theoretical knowledge children are unable to understand how the world around them has come into being. In the words of Marcus Cicero, "To be ignorant of what occurred before you were born is to remain always a child."[60] Theoretical knowledge defines our humanity because it enables us to surpass the practical and the subjective. Only through abstractions from everyday experience, and from a given social context, can we begin to see connections that are imperceptible at the concrete and personal levels. How else could we comprehend the force of gravity or social relations of capitalism? Through abstract concepts and the relationships between phenomena it is possible to derive systems of behavior or meaning, which allow for comprehension of the past and present, as well as projection into the future. Theoretical knowledge is by definition social; it has been produced by a society or community of scholars. Individuals do not generate theoretical knowledge alone, but work from the insights of predecessors and in collaboration with colleagues to arrive at collective understanding, or sometimes conflicting theories. This means that new knowledge is not just discovered—it is derived from and extends already existing knowledge. This is why it is essential that each generation acquires this existing knowledge, to the best of their ability.

Two important educational theorists Émile Durkheim and Lev Vygotsky viewed the passing on of theoretical knowledge to the next generation as the primary purpose of education.[61] The curriculum consists of the knowledge that society deems important for inducting children into the adult world. This knowledge is therefore also tied to a sense of who we are. It should include the best theoretical insights, great literature, beautiful music and art, an understanding of natural and human history, the sciences, different culture, and world regions (all of which can be both internal to the society or from other cultures). Through an induction into this knowledge and cultural heritage children gain a sense of their place in society, a sense of what it means to be human.

With global education, knowledge is rejected as a means to intellectual understanding and socialization into society. Instead, its place in the curriculum is simply for instrumental purpose: preparing young people for work, to help them to get along, to shape their identity or gain a sense of self-worth. As McGovern found with the teaching of perspectives in England's New History curriculum, "any content will do." Content is just the ass that has to carry the sociological baggage of "skills," "concepts," and "perspectives."[62] Global educators teach about global issues, perspectives, and preparation for work because they feel more at ease with these moral frameworks than the moral basis of subject knowledge that underpins education as well as our human potential.

Notes

1 See National Center on Education and the Economy (2007); White (2004).
2 Levine (2005) p. 1.
3 Hicks (2007b) p. 27.
4 White (2004) p. 179.
5 Furedi (2009).
6 Morgan (2006) p. 276.
7 Ibid. p. 279.
8 Ibid. p. 283.
9 United Nations, "Millennium Development Goals." Accessed: http://

www.un.org/millenniumgoals/

10 Ibid. p. 1.

11 Reading International Solidarity Center, *Growing Bananas: A Simulation about Fair Trade for KS 2-3*, 2005. p. 1.

12 Ibid. p. 2.

13 Wisconsin Department of Public Instruction (2002) p. 34.

14 Department for Education and Skills (2005) p. 5.

15 Ibid. p. 5.

16 Wisconsin Department of Public Instruction (2002) p. 22.

17 Garforth *et al.* (2006).

18 Brown University (2011) *The Choices Program: History and Current Issues for the Classroom*. Accessed: http://www.choices.edu/

19 Senechal (2010) p. 15.

20 OFSTED (2011) p. 10.

21 Muller (2000) pp. 65–6.

22 Graves (2003) p. 303.

23 Camicia and Saavedra (2009) p. 513.

24 Ledda (2007) p. 17.

25 Ibid. p. 18.

26 Ibid. p. 18.

27 Pike and Selby (2000). *In the Global Classroom* is published in Canada, but is also used in the US and England.

28 Marshall and Arnot (2009) p. 3.

29 Gärdenfors (2007) p. 76.

30 Heilman (2009) p. 33.

31 Wisconsin Department of Public Instruction (2002) p. 34.

32 Department for International Development (2007).

33 Furedi, F. (2011) p. 4.

34 Ibid. p. 1.

35 Cavanagh, S., "World History and Geography Gain Traction in Class," *Education Week*, 21 March 2007, 26 (28), p. 10.

36 Burack (2003) p. 42.

37 Ibid. p. 52.

38 Ibid. p. 42.

39 Ibid. p. 44.

40 Ibid. p. 51.

41 McGovern (2007) p. 63.

42 Ibid. p. 71.

43 Ibid. p. 63.

44 Department for Education and Skills (2002) p. 5.

45 Wade *et al.* (2009) p. 1.

46 National Center for Languages/Association of Language Learning, "Language Trends 2009." Accessed: www.cilt.org.uk

47 Ibid.

48 Ibid.

49 Ibid.

50 Ibid.

51 Dillon, S., "Schools Stop Teaching Foreign Languages – Except Chinese," *New York Times*, 20 January 2010. Accessed: http://www.nytimes.com/2010/01/21/education/21chinese.html?scp=1&sq=%22growth%20in%20chinese%20language%22&st=cse

52 Ibid.

53 Lawes (2007) p. 89.

54 Ibid. p. 86.

55 Wisconsin Department of Public Instruction (2002) p. 22.

56 Ibid. a) pp. 122–3; b) p. 129; c) p. 146.

57 Hicks (2007b) p. 26.

58 Pike (2000) p. 64.

59 Young (2008) p. 5.

60 Cirerco (46 B.C.) Orator, Chapter 34, Section 120. Cicero: Brutus, Orator, trans. H. M. Hubbell, p. 395. Accessed: http://quotationsbook.com/quote/6289/

61 Young (2008).

62 McGovern (2007) p. 79.

4

Global skills

Skills are not independent of knowledge. Indeed, just about any skill is dependent upon a framework of knowledge for developing and applying it. So why separate the two in this book? In recent discussion of the curriculum, skills have come to be treated as important in their own right, and consequently are increasingly divorced from knowledge. Furthermore, there has been an explosion in the range of "skills" suggested for young people to live and work in a global world.

The rise of a skills-based curriculum in both the US and England is connected to the loss of faith in subject knowledge identified in the previous chapter. Today, only a minority still defend the intrinsic value of subject knowledge, while most argue that education must be tied to some instrumental purpose: the economy, citizenship, identity, inclusion, or social mobility, and proceed to identify the requisite skills that should be taught. As the Royal Society of Arts asserts "we are still educating people for a world that is disappearing."[1] In the authors' view, "the education system of the future must equip individuals to meet the challenges that will face them in managing their lives and their work."[2] In the introductory chapter, we noted the same sentiment echoed by the US Partnership for 21st Century Skills, which identified a gap between the knowledge and skills presently being taught in schools and those that are needed in the twenty-first century.[3]

Both these opinions imply that the current subject-based curriculum, with its emphasis on knowledge about the past and present, is somehow not relevant for the needs of children today. But without knowledge (subject or vocational knowledge) one

cannot develop anything but mundane skills. Global skills are neither intellectual skills nurtured through a general education, nor are they specific vocational skills needed for entering a profession in medicine, engineering, computing, construction, or mechanics, for example. Rather, the "skills" proposed as essential to the success of young people in the twenty-first century include a long list of learning skills and personal, social, and emotional skills (Table 4.1). Keen-eyed readers will notice that many of these skills are in fact competencies, attitudes, dispositions, and behaviors: in other words, they are not skills at all. As such, the rise of global skills in the curriculum not only undermines academic education, but also represents an impoverished view of vocational education (defined here as studying to follow a particular career).

Table 4.1 Global skills in US and English curricula

Learning Skills	Personal, Social, and Emotional Skills
Self-direction	Communication
Critical thinking	Foreign languages
Information and media skills	Teamwork and collaboration
Technology skills	Cross-cultural understanding
Problem solving	Leadership
Creativity	Responsibility to and respect for others
Productivity and accountability	Empathy
Flexibility and adaptability	Social responsibility and citizenship
Learning to learn	Global awareness
Systems thinking	Health awareness
Making judgments, decisions, reasoning	Financial management
Working independently	

This chapter will begin by exploring the expansion of skills being taught to enhance young people's employability in the global market, before looking at personal, social, and emotional skills (skills for global citizenship) as a growth area of the curriculum in the US and England. Again, there is considerable overlap between the two approaches to skills.

Skills for global employment

A central part of the rationale for global education is that we have moved from a world of national economies to a global market economy, a transition that has led to economic restructuring, fundamentally altering the skills-set needed by employees for the jobs being performed in developed economies. Both in America and in England, policy makers and politicians have argued that we are now part of a new global or *knowledge* economy, which demands a higher level of skills and knowledge of employees than a traditional economy with a large manufacturing sector. "[I]n a knowledge economy, education is the new currency by which nations maintain economic competitiveness and global prosperity," pronounces US Secretary of Education, Arne Duncan.[4] The argument is that the outsourcing of manufacturing and some services to developing countries has reduced the need for repetitive, low-skilled work in the West, and the comparative advantage of developed economies is to concentrate on high-end and high-skilled work that other countries cannot do. Countries such as the US and England are discussed in term of a postindustrial economy in which *knowledge* rather than *labor* is the key to success. As former Education Secretary David Blunkett explained in a report to the English Parliament titled *The Learning Age: A Renaissance for a New Britain*, "learning is the key to prosperity – for each of us as individuals, as well as for the nation as a whole."[5]

A report of the New Commission on the Skills of the American Workforce asserts that global companies need employees who are "comfortable with ideas and abstractions, good at both analysis and synthesis, creative and innovative, self-disciplined and well organized," as opposed to disciplined workers performing repetitive tasks.[6] They will also need to be orientated toward global trade and comfortable working with people from other cultures.

Given that economic restructuring is central to the economic rationale for global education, let us examine just how far employment needs have altered. Then we will consider whether and how schools should respond to these changes.

First, it is inaccurate of globalization theorists to portray the global economy as something new. Capitalist economic relations have always been deterritorialized, and economies have been internationally integrated, to a greater or lesser extent, since the midnineteenth century.[7] "The social relations which actually constitute the phenomena which so impress the globalization theorists were already at work in the industrial revolution in England," recalls Justin Rosenberg.[8] In *The Follies of Globalization Theory*, Rosenberg uses the example of the early nineteenth-century "British" cotton industry to explain how early capitalist relations transcended space. Cotton was grown and picked in the American South by relocated African slave-labor, manufactured in factories of Lancashire, with the finished product being sold across Europe and, later, India. Distant people were placed into a relationship with one another; a relationship mediated through commodities. In the final decades of the nineteenth century, rapid imperialist expansion and international division of labor have led some to label this period as the *Belle Époque* or, with the benefit of hindsight, the first era of globalization. For some countries (UK, France, Holland, Japan) international trade relative to domestic trade was equivalent or proportionally higher at the beginning of the twentieth century than it was at the end.[9] Rosenberg suggests that the best that today's globalization theorists can muster is to point to increasing international integration or an accentuation of certain conditions, rather than some qualitative characteristics which could define a new Global Age. The distinction between a labor- and a knowledge-based economy is also a false one as knowledge is a product of labor. It does not just arrive out of thin air. In the end, all of the factors of the "global economy" have been in evidence for many decades.

What has changed is that more countries have liberalized their trading restrictions and formed larger trading blocks and more partnerships, increasing international trade and investment.[10] This liberalization, combined with improved international communication, has facilitated outsourcing from developed to developing countries to exploit cheaper labor and expand markets.

Together with computerization, outsourcing has eliminated millions of blue-collar and administrative support jobs in the US.[11] However, there has been an expansion of other low-skilled job opportunities in service work, sales, technical work, professional occupations, and managerial and administrative work.[12] So while in the 1950s fifty per cent of the workforce was employed in lower-paid, lower-skilled service, leisure, and production jobs, by 2003 that had increased to 75 per cent.[13] American manufacturing remains a significant, if smaller, part of the economy, but more focused on high-end production in specialized electronics and high technology, including airplane wings and semiconductors.[14]

In the UK the decline of manufacturing has been more pronounced, but over the past decade employment has grown most in the areas of educational assistants, care assistants and home care, marketing and sales, office assistants, information and communication technology manager, and financial managers and chartered secretaries.[15] As in the US, there has been an expansion of jobs that need specialized skills (e.g. information technology, pharmacy), but if there is a shortage of job opportunities, it is clerical and other middle-level jobs that are in short supply rather than low-skilled employment.[16] In her *Review of Vocational Education*, conducted for the Conservative-Liberal Democrat Coalition government in 2011, Alison Wolf observes that the result is an employment structure shaped like an hourglass, with plenty of low- and high-skilled jobs, but not much in between.

Another myth is that in the US and England only people with a degree will find employment. In fact, research has shown that many people are overqualified for their job; in the UK, one study found that "typically between a quarter and a third fall into this category."[17] Part of the reason for this shift is the collapse of the youth employment market and the parallel rush for education. Two decades ago, it was common place for many children to leave English schools at sixteen and begin work or an apprenticeship. Today, nearly all young people are in some form of education or training until at least the age of eighteen. In both countries, more young people are entering higher education than ever before, but many also find full-time employment before they complete their degree. There are, however, shortages of skilled employees in some specific areas: science, high-technology, engineering, and mathematics (referred to as STEM areas). On both sides of the Atlantic, there have been initiatives to encourage more young people into education and training in these areas.

In sum, the main changes to employment patterns in the US and England are the decline of middle-level professional jobs (with expansion of low- and high-skilled opportunities), the collapse of the youth market and simultaneous expansion of education, and increased flexibility in the job market. The increased integration of economies has made employment more reactive to market changes, and so there is some need for young people to have a broader skill-set than in the past. Beyond this observation, there is little to suggest that children need "a very different kind of education than most of us have had,"[18] even if we thought schools should directly respond to economic change. Institutions and courses that are vocational certainly do need to be in-tune with the needs of the market, but the primary aim of schools is academic education, not training. Knowledge of excellent literature, history, biology, or music is not rendered less valuable because of economic restructuring. A cynic might argue that the "knowledge economy" thesis acts as an apology for cramming kids into courses and programs that are often unnecessary, unwanted, and in some instances worthless, and so keeping them out of the labor market.

De-skilling vocational education in England

Discussion of economic re-structuring, a "skills gap," and the subsequent need for educational reform in England dates back to the 1970s and early 1980s. Before this time skills were usually viewed either in terms of high-level educational qualifications and analytical capacities, or "hard" technical abilities necessitating physical dexterity, spatial awareness, and technical know-how.[19] Jonathan Payne recalls that when the 1965 National Plan called for more skilled labor, it had in mind engineers, mathematicians, chemists, physicists, economists, computer programmers, mechanics, and electricians.[20] A turning point was then British prime minister James Callaghan's 1976 speech at Ruskin College, in which he called for closer links between education and industry. The backdrop to his speech and the subsequent government intervention into vocational education were the rising numbers of unemployed youth, for whom it was asserted that the education system was not working.

Subsequently, the Manpower Services Commission was established in the mid-1970s to begin the task of re-tooling young people with requisite "skills" for employability. Initially, it sought to do this through the Youth Opportunities Program and the subsequent Youth Training Scheme, which gave certain children the opportunity to experience the work environment. It was from this point that the concept of skill "was detaching itself from particular occupations and moving far beyond its traditional association with the specific technical facilities of the skilled manual worker," including the attitudes and behavior of youth, suggests Payne.[21] The Youth Training Scheme included 103 generic or transferable "skills," including communication skills, reasoning skills, survival skills, problem solving skills, and social and life skills.[22] Lacking either a theoretical foundation or an attachment to specific technical tasks, these schemes appeared to have more to do with generating compliant workers with "desirable values, attitudes, behaviors, and dispositions" than enhancing their skills.[23]

With the benefit of hindsight, such programs were probably equally motivated by a concern for social control as they were with addressing a skills gap. Nevertheless, in the mid-1980s faith was growing that enhanced skills through education could increase economic productivity. These New Growth Theories were associated with economists such as Paul Romer and Robert Lucas, building on the human capital theory that originated in the 1960s with Theordore Schultz's *The Economic Value of Education* and Gary Becker's *Human Capital: A Theoretical and Empirical Analysis, with Special Reference to Education.*[24]

In 1986, the National Council for Vocational Qualifications was created which, with government backing, set about introducing a National Qualifications Framework of vocational courses and qualifications. These courses were not designed for schools, but they became a model for subsequent vocational courses that were later introduced to schools. Over the next ten years, 794 National Vocational Qualifications (NVQs) were produced, covering 95 per cent of occupations, with the content being controlled by representatives of industry and the government rather than by further education teachers or skilled professionals. Unlike the academic curriculum and accredited apprenticeship schemes, which are knowledge-based, NVQs are outcomes-based. Instead of specifying what the pupils should study, NVQs are constructed around the tasks that future employees would need to be able to perform in the workplace. With this outcomes-based approach, skills (derived from knowledge) were replaced with competencies, the ability to perform a task. Pupils had to demonstrate competence, but not an understanding of the tasks they were performing, nor how different tasks relate to each other. NVQs were specifically designed to be nontheoretical for pupils who struggled with learning academic subjects. Hence, there was a conscious attempt to keep assessment practical, not written and theoretical, so as not to disadvantage individuals with poor literacy skills.

NVQs were unpopular with instructors and trainees alike. Professor of Education Alison Wolf suggests that NVQs were despised for their preoccupation with "trivial skills at the expense of knowledge and theory."[25] Most of the initial NVQs, which were geared toward specific professions, were not taken by pupils, many of whom recognized the fluctuating job market and did not want to become tied to one trade. By 2005, Wolf notes that half of NVQs were unwanted and unused, and just 42 (out of 794) awards accounted for 83 per cent of NVQ awards.[26] The successful NVQs were those that closely replicated craft awards previously established by the City and Guilds qualifications. Because of the initial poor uptake of NVQs, General National Vocational Qualifications (GNVQs) were introduced, in areas such as Business, Health, and Leisure and Tourism. However, in making these qualifications more general they were also more abstract and hence academic, suggests Wolf. Unlike NVQs, GNVQs, as a distinctive "vocational" program were taught in secondary schools. Initially, this was for postsixteen education; yet, over the past decade, vocationally related courses have been expanded for fourteen to sixteen year olds as well. Although in 2003 few pupils of this age took such courses, today over 500,000 pupils are enrolled.[27]

The *Review of Vocational Education* finds that there are many successful and innovative vocational programs offered in schools and colleges of further education. But at the same time, some 350,000 16–19 year olds get little to no benefit from the postsixteen education system. These young people are in low-level vocational qualifications that "currently have little or no apparent labor market value."[28] An example of a low-level "vocational" qualification is the Certificate in Preparation for Working Life. The subject content of this qualification falls under the following headings: Personal Awareness, Healthy Lifestyles for Work-Life Balance, Relationships and the Differences Between People, The Changing World of Work, Applying for Jobs and Careers, Economic and Financial Aspects of Life, Employment Opportunities, Enterprise Activities, and Hazard Identification at Home, on the Roads and at Work.[29] In the detailed description, it is clear that the content of the course mixes practical advice (how to write letters of application and a curriculum vitae), mundane information about everyday life (different methods of business payment, identifying different types of formal relationship, and how personal relations can affect work), therapeutic techniques (emotional awareness), and moral advice (how to live a healthy lifestyle). While it is no bad thing for pupils to learn how to apply for a job, the National Qualifications Framework designates this course as equivalent to academic GCSEs. But mastering practical activities and everyday knowledge is far less demanding than learning a foreign language, a science, or history.

The failure to offer pupils either challenging academic study or genuine training for a career has arisen "not despite but *because* of central government's constant redesign, reregulation and reorganization of 14–19 education," suggests Wolf.[30] However, it is not just vocational qualifications that have been transformed by the intervention of the government and the business community. In England, qualifications have also been a driver of change for the academic curriculum as well.[31] The desire to establish "parity of esteem" between vocational and academic qualifications illustrates that the New Labour government and some business leaders thought more highly of their skills curriculum than they did of subject knowledge. Thus, it was only a matter of time before "key skills" were introduced into the academic curriculum so that no child would be without them. Following Ron Dearing's *Review of Qualifications for 16-19 Year Olds* (1996) new key skills specifications were piloted and in 2000 the first pupils began taking courses in key skills. According to Qualifications and Curriculum Authority (QCA):

> Key skills are intended for everyone, from pupils in schools to Chief Executives in large companies. Key skills are the skills most commonly needed for success in a range of activities at

work, in education and training and life in general. They focus candidates' attention on where and how they are using skills for the purpose of improving the quality of their learning, work and performance.[32]

The specifications for key skills covered six areas: communication, application of number, information technology, working with others, improving your own learning, and problem solving. But, as we will explore below with America's skills movement, skills can only be developed in the context of knowledge. Divorced from context, what do skills such as communication and problem solving mean? This conundrum was not lost on Richard Pring:

> Communication (and similarly problem solving) is not that kind of thing. It involves skills certainly - a massive number of them which cannot be reduced to a small number of statements - but involves much more than that, namely sensitivity to different contexts (a good communicator at Old Trafford [football stadium] may be pretty poor at the Athenaeum [the academy of learning]), empathy with different sorts of people, an extensive vocabulary representing conceptual complexity, a grasp of different uses of language, and so on.[33]

Without context, skills of communication or problem solving are so broad that they mean little. A similar conclusion was reached by Joanna Williams in a study of two government policy documents *Success for All* (2002) and *21st Century Skills* (2003). Williams found that the language used by the government to describe skills illustrates their commitment to furthering the twin objectives of economic success and social inclusion. In other words, the New Labour government viewed skills as a path to employment and community participation, not education. An outcome of this instrumentalist approach, suggests Williams, is that skills are treated like a commodity, "a tangible product," that has become separated from the person.[34] The result in an impoverished and commodified vision of education and a tendency to treat it as a transaction or investment, rather than something to explore and master. Competencies and basic skills may be measurable and a way to hold teachers "accountable," but that does not make them necessarily of worth to pupils. "The problem here is not with teaching basic skills, but the fact that teaching anything *beyond* basic skills is called into question," [author's italics] concludes Williams.[35]

A further problem with the skills-based approach adopted under New Labour is that "the 'blame' for poor employment prospects is clearly shifted away from governments and on to individuals" observes Williams.[36] If you don't have a job or live in poverty then this is because you have not developed the skills employers are looking for rather than the decline of middle-level jobs identified above.

While government has evidently played a key role in the hollowing out of vocational and academic education, they are not the only ones at fault. Ultimately, the failure to value either academic or vocational knowledge means that education has been reduced to preparation for everyday living, and a form of therapy, as we will discuss further below. The more control over the vocational, and academic, curriculum has been wrested from communities of specialists and into the hands of the government and bureaucrats, the further it has moved from its own moral purpose.

Twenty-first-century skills for American students

The discussion of twenty-first-century skills in America echo's the development of key skills in England. "Twenty-first century skills . . . are the lifeblood of a productive workforce in today's global, knowledge-based economy," asserts Susan D. Patrick, director of educational technology at the US Department of Education.[37] As in England, these "twenty-first century skills" turn out to be very similar to skills that have been promoted by advocacy groups in the past. At the beginning of the twentieth century, progressive educators and industrialists were calling for a curriculum that would "adapt education to the real life and real needs" of children. In fact, Diane Ravitch identifies "A Century of Skills Movements."[38] In the 1920s and 30s, the activity movement encouraged "solving real-life problems like how to build a playhouse" as well as decision-making and cooperative group learning.[39] In the 1950s, there was the Life Adjustment Movement, in the 1980s, Outcomes-Based Education, and in the 1990s, the Secretary's Commission on Achieving Necessary Skills. Common to all these movements was the antiintellectual sentiment of both progressives and industrialists. Despite the voices of advocates for a practical and personal curriculum throughout the twentieth century, the 1980s was the decade when, politically, a connection was established between declining productivity in the American economy and falling educational standards in classrooms. In the US case, the publication of *A Nation at Risk: The Imperative for Educational Reform,* a report of the National Commission on Excellence in Education, in 1983, launched a debate about economic growth as a goal for education. Since this time schools have emphasized vocationally related skills of literacy, data handling, personal organization, teamwork, study habits, and problem solving in their curricula. It also set in the minds of the American public the idea that education was the key to economic productivity, for both individuals and the nation. For a nation that was already orientated toward individual achievement, the significance of education to personal life success was heightened.

The predecessor to today's influential Partnership for 21st Century Skills (P21) was the CEO Forum, comprising representatives from Computer Systems Policy Project, the National Education Association, and several technology companies. It began life in 1996, shortly after Bill Clinton announced his plan to connect all schools to the Internet. In 2002, P21 replaced the CEO Forum with an expanded membership, including many of America's leading technology companies (Chapter 2) as well as backing from the US Department of Education. Over recent years, P21 has gained significant momentum, with sixteen states signing up to teach its skills framework. The framework consists of learning skills, interdisciplinary themes, and core subjects (the traditional curriculum). The "learning skills" include information and media literacy skills, communication skills, critical thinking and systems skills, problem identification, formulation and solution, creativity and intellectual curiosity, interpersonal and collaborative skills, self-direction, accountability and adaptability, and social responsibility. The interdisciplinary themes are global awareness, financial, economic, business, and entrepreneurial literacy and civic literacy.

Examples of P21 Activities:

- *Fourth-grade Social Studies Lesson:* "work in small groups to discuss problems that they have observed or heard about in their school such as bullying or graffiti. Convening as a whole class, students should come to some common agreement about the problems that are most meaningful. After the problem has been selected by mutual consent, students take responsibility for specifying elements of an inquiry into the causes and possible solutions to the problem."[40]

- *Twelfth-grade English Lesson:* "students translate a piece of dialogue from a Shakespearean play into a text message exchange and analyze the effect of the writing mode on the tone or meaning of the dialogue. Students then discuss audience and purpose in relation to communication media."[41]

Such activities may well engage pupils in problem solving and communication, but what will they learn from the lessons? In the fourth-grade lesson, they will probably generate some ideas for policing each other's behavior. In the second example, pupils might be challenged to extend their texting vocabulary and they might see that genre is influenced by the choice of words, but they will not learn anything about Shakespeare's writing nor the historical context that influenced his writing.

The initial P21 framework did not include subject disciplines. But after some public criticism of the failure to include subject knowledge in their plans, subjects were added for good measure.[42] So while P21 now incorporates academic subjects, the framework given to their study "disregards the structured study, discipline, and concentration that such mastery entails."[43]

In contrast to P21 skills, which were much more clearly corporate-driven, the Common Core State Standards contain skills needed for education: reading, writing, speaking, presenting, numeracy, data handling and so forth. For instance, fourth graders are expected to: "Read on-level prose and poetry orally with accuracy, appropriate rate, and expression on successive readings."[44] And eighth graders should be able to: "Present information, findings, and supporting evidence, conveying a clear and distinct perspective, such that listeners can follow the line of reasoning, alternative or opposing perspectives are addressed, and the organization, development, substance, and style are appropriate to purpose, audience, and a range of formal and informal tasks."[45]

While it may be helpful for teachers to break complex tasks like reading and mathematical operations down into a progression of smaller skills this ignores the contextual knowledge upon which they depend. It shows that the authors of these standards see language and mathematics as skills, not areas of knowledge: "English-language arts and math were the first subjects chosen for the common core state standards because these two subjects are skills, upon which students build skill sets in other subject areas. They are also the subjects most frequently assessed for accountability purposes."[46] The statement that English and mathematics are "skills" rather than subjects with a specialized knowledge base indicates that these standards are not so far away from those produced by the Partnership for 21st Century Skills. Both avoid the question of the knowledge that children need to learn to read with comprehension and understand mathematical operations. The Common Core State Standards do at least acknowledge the need for aligning skills with content knowledge: "To be effective in improving education and getting all students ready for college, workforce training, and life, the Standards must be partnered with a content-rich curriculum and robust assessments, both aligned to the Standards."[47] The document also includes texts illustrating the range of reading at each grade level, with classics such as *Charlotte's Web*, *Alice in Wonderland*, and *Huckleberry Finn*. But it is telling that this list is an appendix to the skills standards, suggesting that content is used to develop skills rather than skills helping pupils to access knowledge.

The mistake made by promoters of "twenty-first century skills" or "common core skills" is to treat skills as something separate from knowledge, or as a functional outcome of knowledge, thereby missing the fact that, as psychologist Daniel Willingham explains, "The processes of thinking are intertwined with the content of thought (that is, domain knowledge)."[48] This means that when we are learning a skill, like reading comprehension, how well we do depends upon how much we already know about the subject we are reading about. Most adults would comprehend a piece of text on gardening or cooking, given that these topics will involve concepts and ideas with which they will likely be familiar, but a text about particle physics or molecular biology will present more of a challenge to most. Unless one has some background knowledge of the concepts being discussed, comprehension will be limited. Of course, through reading such texts, knowledge can be developed and comprehension improved. But the point is that most skills are specific to the domain of knowledge in which they are developed. "Could Steven Spielberg manage the Yankees?" asks E. D. Hirsch Jr., to which his answer is a resounding "No": "The how-to elements of creativity, problem solving, language comprehension, and critical thinking are far, far less important than domain-specific knowledge."[49] Although, as we will see below, higher-order cognitive skills developed in one context can be applied in analogous situations.

It is for this reason that Willingham questions whether it is indeed possible to teach a skill like critical thinking, and is skeptical of courses that claim to teach it. He notes that what such courses often do is teach pupils metacognitive strategies and attitudes that are important for thinking critically, such as reasoning, making judgments, weighing evidence, seeing both sides of an issue, being open to new ideas, and making inferences from available facts. These are important, but without deep structural knowledge, they are limited. "Meta-cognitive strategies only tell the students what they should do – they do not provide the knowledge that students need to actually do it."[50] Willingham uses the example of conducting experiments to illustrate how the ability to think critically and creatively with respect to interpreting the results and controlling the parameters of experiments are intimately tied to one's prior knowledge:

> Data that seem odd because they don't fit one's mental model of the phenomena under investigation are highly informative. They tell you that your understanding is incomplete, and they guide the development of new hypotheses. But you could only recognize the outcome of an experiment as anomalous if you had some expectation of how it would turn out. And that expectation would be based on domain knowledge, as would your ability to create a new hypothesis that takes the anomalous outcome into account.[51]

This is a similar conundrum to that which we encountered in the previous chapter with regard to global issues. The emphasis was placed upon engagement with issues, but often children lacked the background knowledge to understand the problem, and hence their solutions were pretty meaningless. With both approaches, process is elevated over content.

The outcome of separating content (knowledge) from process (skills) is to reduce learning to mundane and trivial everyday tasks of little educational value.

How do schools and colleges prepare young people for work?

For a moment, let us suspend the question of whether it is the job of schools to prepare young people for employment and ask, which knowledge and skills (and attitudes and dispositions) do today's employers value and how does one acquire them? This will of course vary from job to job. Many low-skilled jobs require only basic literacy and numeracy, as well as the ability to communicate with others, while high-skilled jobs demand specialist knowledge and skills. As a general list, employers today value: competency in reading, writing, arithmetic, and communication as well as higher level thinking skills of research, analysis, synthesis, evaluation, problem solving, and decision-making.[52] As the above examples show, such skills are developed through the acquisition of knowledge.

In applying oneself to master difficult areas of knowledge, children develop positive attitudes and dispositions. Another way that these skills can be acquired is through work. Through apprenticeships or job training employers help trainees to learn the particular skills needed to perform a job as well as the dispositions conducive to work. Of course different skills are needed for performing manual and skilled work, but employees become better at performing problem solving, research, evaluation, and decision-making in their given area of expertise the more experienced they become. Hence, employers also value work experience, because "a genuine workplace teaches both general and specific work-skills more effectively than any education-based simulation can."[53] This points toward the need for a much-improved system of vocational education and training than presently exists in both America and England.

However, Alison Wolf argues that prior to work, the best *general* vocational training is academic education as provided by a subject-based curriculum. She suggests that the academic curriculum, "including maths, analytical writing, and comprehension of complex prose - is not only very general in its likely relevance but suited to just that expanding category of professional and technical jobs that we want for ourselves and our children."[54] What makes it suited to high-skilled professional and technical jobs is less its content than the fact that learning indepth subject knowledge develops a pupil's "capacity for thinking, knowing, reflecting, imagining, observing, judging, and questioning."[55] Although such skills are developed through specific subject knowledge, the skilled individual will be able to apply them to solve problems in other knowledge domains. Therefore, "employers opt for the academically educated; and the educated land the good jobs."[56] Wolf notes that for most employers, academic qualifications both act as a proxy measure of ability and recognition of desirable concrete skills and attitudes learned, such as perseverance, personal organization, motivation, reading comprehension, writing fluency and accuracy, and mathematical ability.

As the market for youth employment has steadily declined in England and the US, young people are spending more years in education, but often because education is viewed as a means to employment or because they have little choice, rather than a desire to learn. Many also use community colleges (in the US) or vocational courses (in England) as a stepping stone to higher education. Unfortunately, the push to open up higher education to more young people has been achieved not by raising more people to a higher academic level, but by a reduction in the intellectual requirements. In a survey of student time use from the 1920s to today, Philip Babcock and Mindy Marks found that currently enrolled full-time college students on average report spending only twenty-seven hours per week on academic activities, which is less time than a typical high school student spends at school.[57] From the 1920s to the 60s, the equivalent figure for study and class time was forty hours. One would expect that, with reduced study, grades would suffer. But Richard Arum and Josipa Roksa report that, in many cases, students receive "high marks and make steady progress towards their college degrees" with "limited academic effort" and that faculty and administration are complicit in lowering the academic bar.[58] This means, ironically, that the qualifications upon which universities, colleges, and employers have depended for so long are no longer effective measures of those qualities they seek in young people. With teachers spending less time on challenging subject knowledge, the academic curriculum has become less demanding for pupils. Consequently, employers and higher education institutions demand ever-higher levels of qualifications, even though they are worth less and less. For many young people, the rush to education has become more a means of survival than a quest for knowledge and skills, making them "slaves" to the global economy, suggests one author.[59]

In the widest sense, schools should—and do—prepare children for the world of work: socially, mentally, and through the knowledge and skills they impart. But employability is not the purpose of education, and in making it an instrumental aim of schooling, policy makers are undermining both academic and vocational education. As we have seen, when skills are not embedded in the context of learning a subject or career, they are reduced to mundane and banal everyday activities. Teaching a "skills" curriculum is also "counterproductive in economic terms, in that it tends to produce a less capable workforce."[60] In order better to meet the needs of employers and youth, we need rigorous academic *and* vocational paths for students, as well as a clear separation between the two. Schools should offer all children an academic education, after which some may choose to go on to higher education while others will want to train for a career.

Skills for global citizenship

Skills for global citizenship include personal, social, and emotional skills, skills for community participation and citizenship, and learning skills (Table 4.1). The main advocates for this skill-set are global progressive educators and nonprofits. Again, there is considerable overlap between these skills and those promoted by employers. The main difference for global progressives is that the skills they emphasize are developed in the context of exploring global issues, global knowledge, and global ethics, which leads to some differences of emphasis and values. Also, given the ethical rationale behind global citizenship, many of these global skills are tied to global ethics—the topic of the next chapter.

Personal, social, and emotional skills

Personal, social, and emotional skills can be subdivided into practical living skills, skills for managing relationships, and skills for psychological well-being. As we saw above, when skills become divorced from theoretical knowledge, they tend to focus on the practical aspects of life and everyday social problems. Two such areas are financial planning and health. Thus, in the Partnership for 21st Century Skills framework there is a theme devoted to Financial, Economic, Business, and Entrepreneurial Literacy. As part of this theme pupils are expected to achieve the following:

- Knowing how to make appropriate personal economic choices,
- Using entrepreneurial skills to enhance workplace productivity and career options.[61]

Such aims reduce understanding the discipline of mathematics to mundane everyday tasks such as how to balance a check-book, plan a monthly budget, and give the correct change to someone.

There are a number of global skills associated with managing relationships. These include how to deal with bullying, conflict resolution, collaboration and negotiation, the ability to compromise and be flexible, communication (including foreign languages), and the ability to respect the beliefs and values of others. Mostly, these skills are predicated upon the type of individual that global educators are seeking to nurture. This is an individual who values cooperation over competition, is nonjudgmental of different cultures and viewpoints, listens to others rather than asserting their position, and affirms rather than critiques the contributions of others. This skills set then is closely tied to the ethical standpoint which informs global education and will be discussed in the next chapter. Here, a few examples illustrate how such skills are promoted in classrooms.

The first example, Cooperation! (Box 4.1) is taken from Oxfam's *Global Citizenship: The Handbook for Primary Teaching* in England. It draws upon the poster of The Two Mules from *Quaker Peace and Social Witness* to deliver a simple message that cooperation is better than conflict.

BOX 4.1   COOPERATION![62]

*A*im: To encourage pupils to think about how difficulties can
be resolved through compromise and cooperation.
*Put a PE hoop on the floor, and ask two children to stand in
it facing opposite directions. Put one apple on each side of the
hoop, just out of reach. Ask the children inside the hoop to hold
hands, pull in opposite directions, and try to reach their apple.
Then ask other pupils to suggest why this is not a good idea, and
how the children in the hoop could each reach their apples in a
more cooperative way. The most obvious way is for the children
to move together to pick up the apple first from one side and
then from the other.*

Reproduced from *Global Citizenship: The Handbook for
Primary Teachers* (2002) with the permission of Oxfam GB,
Oxfam House, John Smith Drive, Cowley, Oxford OX4 2JY, UK
www.oxfam.org.uk/education. Oxfam GB does not necessarily
endorse any text or activities that accompany the materials.

Another example of an activity designed to promote cooperative
and problem-solving skills is River Crossing, designed by a primary
school teacher from Newcastle-upon-Tyne in the UK. In this lesson
(Box 4.2) children have to cross an imaginary river using only their
hands or feet, as determined by the teacher (some pupils are only
allowed to use their hands, others only their feet). The activity is
suggested for elementary level pupils and it is suggested that it be
followed up with discussion questions about how the task was
successfully completed, the need to work together, and how the
children were feeling during and after the activity.

A third activity, "A Special Friend," is also taken from Oxfam's
primary education handbook (Box 4.3). The objective of this lesson
is for pupils "to have an awareness of others in relation to themselves,
appreciate that their actions have consequences, and show concern
for others in their immediate circle."[63] It is suggested that the activity
be based around any book that illustrates friendship. In the context
of relating to friends, this lesson is focused on desirable personal
qualities and behaviors.

BOX 4.2   RIVER CROSSING[64]

Students sit in a circle and each is given a card. The teacher explains that the long line of mats is a river that everyone has to cross. If a student has a card with a picture of crossed-out feet, she must cross the river without putting her feet in the water; similarly, if a student's card shows crossed-out hands, he cannot put his hands in the water. The teacher asks for suggestions on how to get everyone across and selects students to try each one. When it is established that they need to be helped or to help others if everyone is to get across, the class is given time to work out a plan. The teacher reminds the class that this is not a winner-and-loser activity; success is achieved only when everybody is safely across the river.

Reproduced with the permission of the copyright holder from *In the Global Classroom* 2 copyright © 2000 by Pippin Publishing Corporation.

BOX 4.3   A SPECIAL FRIEND[65]

Read the book with the pupils and then talk about what they do when they are feeling sad or lonely and how class members can help each other at these times. Talk about what makes a friend, what friends do for each other and how to be friendly to new children in the class. Think about particular words to describe friends, about times when we fall out with friends and how to become friends again. Discuss times when pupils like being or want to be on their own. As an extension, pupils could make collages of themselves with their 'special friend', or make a picture for someone special to them.

Reproduced from *Global Citizenship: The Handbook for Primary Teachers* (2002) with the permission of Oxfam GB, Oxfam House, John Smith Drive, Cowley, Oxford OX4 2JY, UK www.oxfam.org.uk/education. Oxfam GB does not necessarily endorse any text or activities that accompany the materials.

Encouraging children to examine their own behavior, values, feelings, and dispositions is seen as a critical part of developing global skills because, in the eyes of global progressives, the development of the psyche and social skills has become the central purpose of education. This leads into the next category of global skills: those to do with psychological well-being.

Psychological well-being

The psychological well-being of children became a central objective in American schools in the late 1980s and the 1990s.[66] At the time, self-esteem was held to be a cure-all to social and academic problems. This shift led to a pedagogical focus on how children were feeling about their lessons rather than their actual accomplishments. "Research shows that promoting social and emotional skills leads to reduced violence and aggression among children, higher academic achievement, and an improved ability to function in schools and the workplace," suggests *Edutopia*, an online education publication.[67] In England, there was a parallel movement from the late 1990s.[68] Here, we show that this therapeutic rationale is central to global education, including skills of self-reflection and affirmation.

The "skill" of reflection "has come to play an integral part in the learning process for both teachers and me," noted global education campaigner Merry Merryfield.[69] Similarly, Gaudelli suggested that, "Education and identity have become nearly synonymous over the past decade."[70] Merryfield has a lesson called the Tree of Life in which the tree is an analogy for the experiences and circumstances that have shaped one's values and beliefs. Merryfield begins by showing children her tree:

> The 'roots' of the tree are family values, early experiences, and one's heritage – e.g. ethnic, religious, socioeconomic, regional. The trunk is made up of experiences from childhood through high school that one perceives as significant in the development of a world-view. Each limb represents an adult experience or action that has modified one's view of other people or the world.[71]

Merryfield then proceeds to ask the pupils to reflect upon their own lives and construct their own trees identifying the "underlying values, beliefs, and experiences that have shaped their views of other people and the world."[72] Undoubtedly, completing such an activity would help one to identify the formative experiences and influences in one's life. As Merryfield surmises, a key outcome of the activity is "their reflections on what they learned about themselves and the process of perspective taking."[73]

Learning skills

Progressive educators have long emphasized child-centered *learning* over teacher-centered *teaching*. While teaching is portrayed as an adult imposition on the child, learning is seen as the individual constructing their own reality. In the classroom, teaching and learning should go hand-in-hand. Teachers structure the knowledge and skills that pupils need to learn such that they can progress from a lower to a higher level of understanding. This is the case whether the teaching method is didactic or enquiry-based. However, the more global the aims for the curriculum, the further education moves away from teaching knowledge and toward a focus on the learning process itself.

An example of learning skills comes from a chart produced by ActionAid: *Get Global! A Skills-Based Approach to Active Global Citizenship* (Table 4.2). In this example, the focus of learning is upon the personal skills and confidence of the child rather than the object of study; in other words, not *what* they are learning, but learning to learn. "Many proponents of learning to learn appear to regards the emotional outlook, attributes and skills associated with them as more important than subject content," note Ecclestone and Hayes.[74]

Not all learning skills are as banal as those listed in the above example. When pupils investigate a real-world problem in a specific cultural and political context, a number of research skills need to be employed to effectively complete this task. These include skills of searching for information, selecting and processing information, analysis, comparison, synthesis, and evaluation. A good source for illustrating these learning skills is the *Global Education Checklist*

Table 4.2   Global learning skills chart[75]

Low score	(1 2 3 4 5 6) High score
Lost confidence	Gained Confidence
Worked on my own with difficulty	Worked on my own with ease
Found working with a group difficult	Worked easily as part of a group
Found contributing to a discussion difficult	Contributed easily to discussions
Expressed my own opinion with difficulty	Expressed my own opinions easily
Found listening to other people's opinions difficult	Listened to other people's opinions easily
Found challenging opinions difficult	Challenged my own/other people's opinions easily
Did not negotiate well	Negotiated well
Did not make decisions	Made decisions
Did not reflect on ideas	Reflected on ideas
Did not make a difference	Made a difference

Reproduced from *Get Global! A Skills-Based Approach to Active Global Citizenship* (2003) with the permission of ActionAid.

compiled for the American Forum for Global Education. Some examples include:

Global issues:

- Do students know how to look for information about an issue? Do students know how to develop criteria for discriminating, evaluating, selecting and responding to useful and relevant data? Do they know how to process the information that they have found? Do they know how to present their information to others?

Culture:

• Do students know how to analyze and evaluate major events and trends in a culture?

Global connections:

• Can students recognize, analyze, and evaluate major events and trends in American and world history and examine how these events and trends connect to their local communities and the United States?

• Can students recognize, analyze, and evaluate interconnections of local and regional issues with global challenges and issues?

• Can students recognize, analyze, and evaluate the interconnections between their lives and global issues?[76]

This example illustrates that global education sometimes can integrate skills and knowledge in a meaningful way. In order to "analyze and evaluate major events and trends in a culture" or "recognize, analyze, and evaluate interconnections of local and regional issues with global challenges and issues" a lot of knowledge about cultures, countries, and politics is needed. The problem arises when the focus is placed narrowly upon the skills themselves.

Community participation and citizenship

There is a long history of promoting citizenship education, especially in American education. With global education, the framework for these skills has shifted from the nation state to something much more fluid. Hence, the National Council for Social Studies identifies the role of the citizen at the scale of the community, the nation, and the world, while learning about American government has been reduced to one section of the theme "Power, Authority, and Governance." In England, the citizenship national curriculum is introduced with the suggestion that children learn to "play an active role in the life of their schools, neighborhoods, communities and wider society as active and global citizens."[77] Above, ActionAid use global citizenship as its framework to teach skills of cooperation and negotiation.

In the US, Challenge 20/20 is an initiative launched by the National Association for Independent Schools to engage pupils in collaborative work to address global issues. The idea comes from J. F. Rischard's book *High Noon: 20 Global Problems, 20 Years to Solve Them.*[78] The twenty problems include global warming, deforestation, fisheries depletion, education for all, the digital divide, natural disaster prevention and mitigation, illegal drugs, intellectual property rights, and international labor and migration rules. One of the aims is to encourage pupils from different schools to work together to find solutions to the problems.

Undoubtedly, an important part of schooling is learning to interact with others. After all, education is a social pursuit. Collaborative projects, assuming responsibility, collective planning and organization, and community participation are all worthwhile activities and something that most schools encourage. However, they are not *the curriculum*. Education may necessitate engaging with others, but its purpose is to bring clarity of understanding to the objects of study. The danger with global learning is that personal and social skills are treated as valid ends of education, and in doing so education becomes less challenging, less intellectual, less interesting, and ultimately less meaningful.

Conclusion

Not surprisingly, skills for global citizenship and learning suffer the same shortcomings as skills for the global marketplace. Both reduce skills developed through knowledge to context-less and mostly trivial competencies. They both also tend to fetishize competencies as ends of education, rather than a means to knowledge and understanding. Global skills revise the meaning of education as preparation for work and life.

Introducing vocationally related skills into the mainstream curriculum transforms schools from institutions of education into institutions of employment training, in the process undermining the professionalism of teachers and lowering educational expectations for children. An economic rationale for the curriculum is not an educational one and hence can only devalue the importance of academic learning. Acquiring the skills, and knowledge, needed for employment should be addressed through a general academic curriculum followed by vocational education tied to careers. "Twenty-first century skills," or "key skills," provide neither academic nor vocational education. If anything, they provide a rationale for *not* educating children.

As illustrated above, the origins of the skills movement reside in nonacademic courses and training for those children who were unfortunately deemed incapable of academic work. Instead, they were to learn competencies, which are about doing rather than knowing. Those advocating global skills, key skills or twenty-first-century skills as part of the mainstream curriculum are today arguing that these are more relevant to the needs of all pupils than an academic education. This movement reflects diminished expectations, a lowering of educational standards, and a belief that the academic curriculum is beyond the reach of many children. A cause that started by asserting the need for a better-trained and more knowledgeable workforce has put forward a curriculum that requires little knowledge and only basic skills.

With personal, social, and emotional skills, education has been reduced to everyday living: managing social relationships, how to organize your finances, how to find information, or manage your own emotions. Here, the focus of education has become learning about the self rather than learning about the world. This means nothing less than the substitution of intellectual aims for the curriculum with psychosocial ones, which encourages individuals to look inward rather than out into the world. The purpose of education is to expand horizons and take individuals beyond their limited personal experiences, not to imprison them in the circumstances into which they were born. For children to be educated they need access to theoretical and abstract knowledge about the world. Equipped with such knowledge, children will become skilled individuals. Without it, they will remain uneducated.

Notes

1   Bayliss (1999) p. 1.
2   Ibid. p. 4.

3   Partnership for 21st Century Skills, "Mission," 2009.
    Accessed: http://www.p21.org/index.php?option = com_
    content&task = view&id = 188&Itemid = 110

4   Duncan, A., U.S. Secretary of Education, "Speech to the UN
    Educational, Scientific and Cultural Organization (UNESCO)," 4th
    November 2010. *Common Core State Standards Initiative*, 2009.
    Accessed: http://www.corestandards.org

5   Blunkett, D., *The Learning Age: A Renaissance for a New Britain*,
    "Foreword," 1998. Accessed: http://www.lifelonglearning.co.uk/
    greenpaper/summary.pdf

6   National Center on Education and the Economy (2007) p. xviii.

7   See Hirst and Thompson (1998); Osterhammel and Peterson (2003).

8   Rosenberg (2000) p. 33.

9   Hirst and Thompson (1998) p. 27.

10 Dicken (2003).

11 Levy and Murnane (2007) p. 164.

12 Ibid. 166.

13 Dicken (2003).

14 Manning, "Is Anything Made in the USA Anymore? You'd be
    Surprised," *New York Times*, 20 February 2009. Accessed: http://
    www.nytimes.com/2009/02/20/business/worldbusiness/20iht-
    wbmake.1.20332814.html

15 Labor Source Survey cited in Wolf (2011) p. 147.

16 Wolf (2011) p. 35.

17 Chevalier & Lindley (2009).

18 National Centre on Education and the Economy (2007) p. xviii.

19 Payne (2000).

20 Ibid. p. 355.

21 Ibid. p. 356.

22 Manpower Service Commission, *Core Skills in YTS Part One: Youth
    Training Scheme Manual*. Sheffield: MSC, 1984.

23 Payne (2000) p. 356.

24 Mullan, P., "Education – It's Not for the Economy, Stupid!" *Spiked-
    online*, 3 August 2004. Accessed: http://www.spiked-online.com/
    Printable/0000000CA640.htm

25 Wolf (2002) p. 80.

26 Ibid. p. 76.

27 Wolf (2011) p. 48.

28 Ibid. p. 31.

29 Assessment & Qualifications Alliance, "Preparation for Working Life: Level 1/Level 2 Specification 4800," 2009. Accessed: http://store.aqa.org.uk/qual/pdf/AQA-4800-W-SP-11.PDF

30 Wolf (2011) p. 21.

31 Young (2008).

32 Qualifications & Curriculum Authority, "The Key Skills Specifications and Guidance," 2002. Accessed: http://www.ngfl-cymru.org.uk/vtc/ngfl/2007-08/key_skills/wjec_2008/13%20Standards/Main%20KS/KS%20Specifications%20and%20Guidance.pdf

33 Pring (1995).

34 Williams (2005) p. 181.

35 Ibid. p. 189.

36 Ibid. p. 185.

37 Patrick, S., "Partnership for 21st Century Skills: Events and News," 2005. Accessed: http://www.p21.org/index.php?option = com_content&task = view&id = 86&Itemid = 64

38 Ravitch, D. (2010b) p. 12.

39 Ibid.

40 Partnership for 21st Century Skills, "Social Studies Map," 2008. Accessed: http://www.p21.org/documents/ss_map_11_12_08.pdf

41 Partnership for 21st Century Skills, "English Map," 2008. Accessed: http://www.p21.org/documents/21st_century_skills_english_map.pdf

42 Sawchuk, S., "Backers of 21st-Century Skills' Take Flak," *Education Week*, 4 December 2009. Accessed: http://www.edweek.org/ew/articles/2009/03/04/23pushback_ep.h28.html

43 Senechal, D. (2010) p. 5.

44 Council of Chief State School Officers & the National Governors Association, *Common Core State Standards for English Language Arts & Literacy in History/Social Studies, Science, and Technical Subjects*, 2010. Accessed: http://www.corestandards.org/assets/CCSSI_ELA%20Standards.pdf

45 Ibid.

46 Council of Chief State School Officers & the National Governors Association, "Common Core State Standards: Frequently Asked Questions," 2010. http://www.corestandards.org/assets/CoreFAQ.pdf

47 Council of Chief State School Officers & the National Governors Association, "Common Core State Standards: Presentation," 2010. http://www.corestandards.org/

48 Willingham (2007) p. 8.

49 Hirsch, E. D., "The 21st Century Skills Movement," Press Release, 24 February 2009. Accessed: http://www.commoncore.org/pressrelease-04.php

50 Willingham (2007) p. 15.

51 Ibid. p. 17.

52 See National Center on Education and the Economy (2007); Levy & Murnane (2007); Wolf (2011).

53 Wolf (2011) p. 33.

54 Wolf (2002) p. 86.

55 Furedi (2009) p. 65.

56 Wolf (2002) p. 86.

57 Babcock and Marks cited in Arum and Roksa (2011) p. 3.

58 Arum and Roksa (2011) p. 5.

59 Laïdi (1998) p. 11.

60 Mullan, P., "Education – It's Not for the Economy, Stupid!" *Spiked-online*, 3 August 2004. Accessed: http://www.spiked-online.com/Printable/0000000CA640.htm

61 Partnership for 21st Century Skills (2009) p. 2.

62 Young (2002) p. 47.

63 Young (2002) p. 60.

64 Pike and Selby (2000) p. 42.

65 Ibid. p. 60.

66 Hunter (2001).

67 Edutopia Staff, "Why Champion Social and Emotional Learning? Because it Helps Students Build Character," *Edutopia*, 30 October 2008. Accessed: http://www.edutopia.org/social-emotional-learning-introduction

68 Ecclestone and Hayes (2009).

69 Merryfield (1993) p. 28.

70 Gaudelli (2003) p. 102.

71 Merryfield (1993) p. 28.

72 Ibid. p. 28.

73 Ibid. p. 30.

74 Ecclestone and Hayes (2009) p. 51.

75 ActionAid, *Get Global! A Skills-Based Approach to Active Global Citizenship, 2003.* Accessed: http://www.actionaid.org.uk/schoolsandyouth/getglobal/pdfs/getglobal.pdf

76 Czarra, F., "Global Education Checklist for Teachers, Schools, School Systems and State Education Agencies." *American Forum for Global Education*, pp. 2–4, 2003. Accessed: http://www.globaled.org/fianlcopy.pdf

77 Qualification and Curriculum Development Authority, "Citizenship Key Stage 3," 2010. Accessed: http://curriculum.qcda.gov.uk/key-stages-3-and-4/subjects/key-stage-3/citizenship/index.aspx

78 Rischard (2003).

5

Global ethics

This chapter explores the moral or ethical case for global education: ethics meaning a set of moral principles or values. Quite simply, advocates of the global ethical framework assert that our society, our commitment to others, our citizenship, and our sense of identity are no longer confined to the boundaries of a national (or other) territory, but rather are global. Hence, global education seeks to go beyond offering knowledge and skills, but to engage children emotionally in a "global" mindset or perspective, so that they identify themselves as global citizens. Global education, then, is a new worldview or framework for understanding our sense of being. As one author explains:

> Global education is not global in the sense of being *all-encompassing*, nor is it synonymous with international or foreign studies. Global education at the elementary level might best be described as a focus of education that facilitates development of the child's sense of himself or herself as a personal and social being.[1]

Today, this definition applies equally well where global education is taught at any level of education. With global ethics, the term 'global' is used less as a geographical reference, meaning worldwide, but rather to depict a different way of understanding ourselves, which necessitates breaking down previous boundaries through which we gained meaning for our lives. This includes barriers between cultures, communities, nations, and areas of knowledge or skills. Thus, global education aims to: "Develop citizens who know how to live and work across cultures and boundaries. . . . Help students remove the barrier between 'self' and 'other' so that they may work and communicate effectively in other cultures and countries."[2]

In challenging the boundaries through which we gain meaning and purpose in society, global ethics rejects previous sources of external authority for education and identity (knowledge and culture). Yet it does not offer an alternative external source of authority: its "moral" framework is the individual self. Education is thus redefined not as access to the authority of distinctive areas of knowledge or a particular culture with a moral framework, but as meaning and identity for individuals derived from "global issues" and "global values." Therefore, global educators do have in mind certain dispositions or values they hope children will embrace, and they design lessons accordingly. "Education constitutes the central pillar of strategies to promote such values" reported the United Nations International Implementation Scheme for the Decade.[3] Derived from a Western, liberal elite, these values include tolerance of multiple perspectives, diversity, human rights, social and environmental justice, participation, peace, interdependence, and respect for the environment. For the most part, it is not the values themselves that are problematic, but the way in which they are employed to circumvent a discussion about the moral basis of our society. Diversity, nonjudgmental tolerance, or respect for the environment do not get us any closer to identifying the human qualities that we value. The global citizen that these values aim to create is an emotivist self who "engages" with global issues, but for the purpose of satisfying the self rather than advancing society.

Identity and self-esteem

Global education started out in the 1960s and 70s with an attachment to alternative social programs. But by its very nature it blurs the boundary between social change and individual change, between reality and mind, between education and politics, as we saw in Chapter 1. With the theory of global citizenship, the one leads to the other. This is why global activists seek to influence the school curriculum, as Crews explains: "As we comprehend existing symbols or create new theoretical constructs to help us explain the world around us, that world changes because our perceptions of it are no longer the same."[4] In Oxfam's *Curriculum for Global Citizenship*, a sense of identity and self-esteem is included in the table of values and attitudes. Oxfam emphasizes "awareness of and pride in individuality," the importance of "individual worth" and "open mindedness."[5] Similarly, in *Global Teacher, Global Learner*, Pike and Selby include a chapter on activities for enhancing self-esteem. Some sample activities include Sunflowers, Affirmation Circles, Feelings Thermometers, and Affirmation Notebooks (Box 5.1).

As belief in large-scale social transformation has waned, global educators have increasingly focused their efforts on nurturing individual identity. This movement has roots in progressive education, whereby, as James Nolan explains, "the telos moved from obedience to externally imposed moral and intellectual demands to realization of internally derived needs and experiences."[6] Yet "internally derived needs and experiences" is not a sound basis for educating children. No child will be able to comprehend mathematics, biology, classical literature, or learn to play a musical instrument or become a great athlete on their own. In order for a child to master difficult skills and gain insight into theoretical knowledge, he or she needs tutelage by a suitably experienced adult. None of these skills and knowledge is acquired easily or quickly. In most cases, they take years of study and practice which demands a high level of discipline and structured learning. In all but the most exceptional cases, the discipline, structure, and the setting of objectives needed to master subjects and high-level skills will be externally imposed. This is the responsibility of the teacher. Where teachers have replaced these tasks with helping children to explore their identity or affirming their self-worth or letting children set their own learning objectives, they are avoiding their responsibilities as educators.

The contemporary concern for identity and self-esteem as pedagogical aims has not been without controversy. As curricular aims, they have been criticized for introducing therapy into the classroom in place of education, for elevating self-realization over external goals,[7] and for failing to make any difference to social problems.[8]

BOX 5.1   GLOBAL TEACHER, GLOBAL LEARNER[9]

Sunflowers

Each student makes a paper sunflower by decorating a paper circle and affixing it to a long stem, to which are attached some leaves. The student's name is written on a leaf, and all the flowers are affixed to the wall. A supply of paper petals should be readily available in the classroom. Whenever a student wants to make an appreciative comment about another student, she writes the comment on a petal and sticks it onto the person's sunflower. Each student's flower is thus built up over a period of time by a range of affirmative statements.

Affirmation circles

Sharing feelings about themselves and others in a circle can be a regular feature of the affirmative classroom. Students sit or stand, holding hands or linking arms if they wish, in a circle, taking it in turns to speak. Topics chosen by the teacher or students might range from 'something nice that happened to me today/ yesterday/at the weekend' or 'right now I feel . . .', to sharing of likes/dislikes and attributes: 'I'm happiest/angriest when . . . .' Participants should not be under any compulsion to contribute and statements are not discussed, though positive support and encouragement can be given by the group.

Feelings thermometer

Each student is given a feelings thermometer—a strip of card onto which faces [each expressing an array of emotions] are pasted. The faces represent happy, sad, silly, mad, scared, and proud feelings. During an Affirmation Circle time, the thermometers can be used to give a quick gauge as to how students individually and collectively feel about certain ideas or experiences: a paper clip or finger is used to indicate the appropriate feeling.

(Continued)

> ### Affirmation notebooks
>
> *This is a personal collection of individual self-affirming sheets which are designed and compiled over a period of a term or year. Sheets can include students' drawings of themselves, personal badges and descriptions, likes and dislikes, earliest memories, family trees, affirmative comments or drawings by other students, personal awards and certificates etc.*
>
> Reprinted from *Global Teacher, Global Learner* (Hodder & Stoughton) with permission of the copyright holders.

Respect for diversity

James Nolan notes that the self-esteem movement has its roots in values clarification exercises and affirmation for diverse cultural groups in 1960s America.[10] We saw in Chapter 3 that, in the context of learning about other cultures, the emphasis placed upon affirming the cultural identity of others often results in superficiality and lack of critical engagement in the curriculum. Cultural groups and minorities are included so that children learn to identify such groups and "respect" their differences, thus affirming their particular identity: but this is not the same thing as understanding culture. Focusing upon symbolic expressions of culture, rather than understanding the ideas, beliefs, values, and traditions that gave rise to a particular culture, means substituting "identity" for "culture." Here, culture is no longer a transcendent social process through which people bring meaning and purpose to their lives, but instead becomes a badge to be worn. In this instance, we can see how education as affirmation of the self inhibits an understanding of our social being.

Over time, the concept of diversity has crossed the Atlantic and expanded beyond culture to include diverse perspectives, diverse environments, and even diverse species (these latter two providing a link to environmental values which are addressed below). The New Labour government illustrated this broad interpretation of the value of diversity in its 2005 publication *Developing a Global Dimension in the School Curriculum*:

Diversity

- Appreciating similarities and differences around the world in the context of human rights,
- Understanding the importance of respecting differences in culture, customs, and traditions and how societies are organized and governed,
- Developing a sense of awe at the variety of peoples and environments around the world
- Valuing biodiversity,
- Appreciating diverse perspectives on global issues and how identities affect opinions and perspectives,
- Understanding the nature of prejudice and discrimination and how they can be challenged and combated.[11]

While it is one thing to live in a tolerant, culturally diverse society, turning diversity into a value is a way of avoiding discussion about what our society believes in and which values it upholds. Diversity and multiculturalism have been embraced by American and English cultural institutions in a desperate attempt to "represent a crisis of values as something positive."[12] "The lack of common values is sexed up as 'cultural pluralism' and divisions within communities are relabeled 'diversity,'" reports Brendan O'Neill.[13] This insight helps to explain why diversity has such an empty ring to it and why it fails to bind society together. A case in point is the European Union's motto "*United in diversity*," which is surely a contradiction in terms.

Tolerance of multiple perspectives

Global perspective means "seeing things through the eyes and minds of others – and it means the realization that while individuals and groups may view life differently, they also have common needs and wants," reports Tye.[14] Global tolerance is identified as an important

value in programs such as Global Classrooms and the Model UN, among others.[15]

Any good teacher will encourage his or her pupils to see a problem or event from different points of view. Abstraction from one's own subjective viewpoint is an essential part of learning how to understand social phenomena at a theoretical rather than a personal level. Such abstraction also allows one to judge the merits of a given opinion or perspective, since it necessitates making a distinction between subjective interests and the wider social picture. Yet, with global education, perspective-taking has become an end of, rather than a means to, understanding. Understanding different perspectives is not the same thing as understanding social and political change. As with the twenty-four perspectives promoted in the English History National Curriculum (Chapter 3), an understanding of the causes and the actors in an unfolding narrative of the past has been substituted by the telling of different people's stories or versions of events.

As we noted in Chapter 3, the meaning of tolerance has been expanded "so that it ends up encompassing the idea of acceptance and respect."[16] However, in order to genuinely respect another perspective one has to engage with it and understand it, even if one disagrees. When tolerance equals "don't judge" the outcome is dismissal and disengagement, both of which imply disrespect for the opinions of others. Affirmation is demanded regardless of whether the views and values of others are worthy. This approach to tolerance is thus morally neutral and has its origins in counseling, not education. The aim of the therapist is frequently to value the client's ideas and feelings, to understand their perspective, rather than to give advice.[17]

The act of judgment is in fact an essential part of tolerance, observes Furedi in his book *On Tolerance: A Defense of Moral Independence*.[18] When we tolerate the opinions of others we have made a prior judgment that we value the right of the individual to undertake their own moral reasoning and also that tolerance is an essential component of democracy, since the dissenting opinion could be the right one. Only by engaging with other perspectives in a critical way, not affirming them regardless, do we acknowledge the potential for common insights into humanity. This common ground is what is missing from tolerance as nonjudgmentalism.

This essential role of tolerance in democratic societies is rarely valued today. In Furedi's words:

> From a liberal humanist perspective, judgment is not simply an acceptable response to other people's beliefs and behavior: it is a public duty. It is through the act of judgment that a dialogue is established between an individual and others.[19]

Of course not all judgment is equally valid. But a mature society is one that deals with morally reprehensible opinions through dialogue rather than silencing them. Education should play a critical role in teaching children to engage with opinions and cultural values that are different from their own. Through moral reasoning they learn to make reasoned and informed judgments; they begin to develop their own moral compass and potential for autonomy. Despite the rhetoric of global citizenship and global ethics, this essential part of a child's education is avoided by the politically correct idea of global tolerance that backs away from moral judgment. Instead, liberal elites and global progressives have reinvented tolerance as a disposition toward moral disengagement. As one social studies teacher observed, the global ethic of tolerance is more likely to instill indifference in children than genuine tolerance: "In trying to suppress what is probably a natural human tendency (to judge), these students are more likely to become morally numb, certainly not 'sensitive' to the 'other.'"[20] In essence, public schools are inhibiting the freedom of conscience of children. So we have come full circle from the aims of Mill and Lock who wanted to protect individual conscience from intrusion by the state.

Empathy

The significance of empathy as a global value is described as follows:

> Empathy means caring. It entails building trust and mutual understanding. Building trust requires a willingness to listen carefully to another person with a sincere desire to hear his or her experiences, perspectives, values, and beliefs, whether these are different from or similar to one's own. An empathetic person can gain a sense of another's positions and feelings. Thus, being

able to empathize makes it possible to begin to communicate and participate across and within new cultures.[21]

Empathy is indeed an important value in human relations, and often an outcome of learning about different people's experiences around the world. Any good education that explores the beauty and perils of both the natural and social worlds is sure to stimulate a host of emotional reactions from children. But with global education's focus on children's identity, empathy has become a required lesson outcome. Instead of being a spontaneous reaction to experiences or learning, children are being coached or conditioned to respond in a particular way. In other words, an education of the emotions is being replaced by an education in prescriptive emotional responses.[22]

This was evident in the lesson plan "Growing Bananas" described in Chapter 3, in which one of the aims was to "enable pupils to empathize with Caribbean banana growers."[23] Another example comes from the UK Geographical Association's "Valuing Places" project. Pupils are asked to "read and think for a moment" about the story of an illiterate man from Kenya who gets into difficulties with his medicine bottle (Box 5.2). The lesson outline suggests that using real people's voices helps pupils to "appreciate, value, and view positively the differences and similarities with their own lives."[24] The lesson has been designed so that children "explore personal

---

BOX 5.2   CHEMJO'S STORY[25]

Sixty year old Chemjor Chapkwony from Kenya never had a chance to learn to read. He tells of the effect that this has had on his life:

'*I fell sick and was taken to hospital, where I was given medicine by the doctor. I took the medicine he gave me and went to find a place to sleep.*

In the morning, the person I was staying with came to look for me and found me unconscious. He took me to hospital. Now when I am given medicine, I am afraid to take it because I cannot read the label. So I am afraid.'

Source: Oxfam website, 2004.

connections" and empathize with the Kenyan man. But what if children do not see any connections between their lives and his? What if they have a different emotional response or no emotional response to reading about his story? They may well have learned something about the problems posed by illiteracy in developing countries, but this was not the purpose of the activity; in failing to make an emotional connection with the Kenyan, they have not achieved the lesson's primary aim.

Social and environmental justice

With origins in the writings of Paulo Freire and bell hooks, teaching for social justice has a long established tradition in American education and a growing one in England. In both countries, social justice has been brought under the umbrella of global education as an ethical approach to learning. According to the UK government report *Developing a Global Dimension in the Curriculum*, social justice in the classroom includes:

- Valuing social justice and understanding the importance of it for ensuring equity, justice, and fairness for all with and between societies,
- Recognizing the impact of unequal power and access to resources,
- Developing the motivation and commitment to take action that will contribute to a more just world,
- Challenging racism and other forms of discrimination, inequity, and injustice.[26]

Learning about social justice involves recognizing incidents of inequality or injustice in societies, being motivated to do something about them, and searching for ways to challenge injustice, inequality, and discrimination. Here, we can see that engaging in social justice follows on from empathizing with people's predicaments, as in the above examples of the illiterate Kenyan or the Caribbean banana farmers. Having clearly crossed a line from education to political activism, it is not surprising to learn that teaching for social justice is controversial.

Social justice can mean teaching about stereotypes and discrimination in the home nation.[27] Today, it is also frequently taught through global issues. For example, schools can apply to participate in Challenge 20/20, the web-based program for involving schools in global challenges, run by the US National Association for Independent Schools (NAIS). The list of twenty global problems include global warming, biodiversity and ecosystem losses, deforestation, water deficits, peacekeeping/conflict prevention/combating terrorism, fighting poverty, education for all, infectious diseases, reinventing taxation, illegal drugs, intellectual property rights, and international labor and migration rules. Pupils from different schools collaborate to address one particular global issue. Some examples of successful projects undertaken in schools are shown in a website video.[28] The video shows pupils at different schools engaged in projects compositing their trash, measuring river pollution, setting up a biodiversity ethics council, and contributing to the Helping Hands program, which distributes hand sanitizer (an antiseptic hand wash) in El Salvador.

Exploring issues such as biodiversity, pollution, and the spread of disease can be a stimulating and challenging educational experience for pupils who have the requisite background knowledge. The open-ended nature of learning about issues means that pupils can explore the topic and take their learning in a number of directions. This makes it an exciting and challenging way to teach, as pupils will need guidance to help them find the answers they are looking for. Learning about the different environmental and social challenges that people face around the world, and being confronted with examples of injustice, is also an important part of schooling. However, such issues are currently popular with teachers who see them as more "relevant" or motivating for children than academic knowledge. "International education combats student disinterest and apathy," report the authors of Wisconsin's *Planning Curriculum in International Education*.[29] This approach also politicizes education; making it not so much about learning knowledge, but instead addressing political issues facing society.

When problems faced by people in other countries are presented as global issues, the tendency is to move away from an attempt to understand the cultural and political context and toward the banal assertion that we are all responsible for the problems of the world. A primary objective is to *engage* children in issues of social or environmental justice: as the NAIS video suggests, the goal is to move pupils "from engagement to reflection to action." Treating children as "citizens" with political responsibility is only possible because the global approach blurs the lines between the public and private spheres. Hence, individual actions, like such as changing one's consumption habits or recycling, have been recast as "political" actions that have significant consequences for changing the world.

Engagement is either a therapeutic or political objective (depending upon whether the outcome is personal change or some kind of political action), but it is not an educational one. This is why teaching for social justice uses the language of "raising awareness" and "a concern for," but rarely talks about knowledge and understanding.

Conflict resolution and peace

Conflict resolution and peace are frequently cited as part of global ethics—although it is debatable whether conflict resolution is an ethic. Global educators are advocating a commitment to peaceful conflict resolution rather than violence, which is an alternative way to resolve conflict. Again, the focus of learning is upon the child's personal values and interpersonal behavior, rather than an exploration of the ethics of human behavior in different places and times. As with the two sample lessons described in Chapter 4, Oxfam's "Cooperation!" and "River Crossing,"[30] the aim is to teach children to cooperate and resolve problems while working together, rather than competing and resorting to conflict.

Such lessons move quickly between a discussion about war and politics to personal values and interpersonal behavior. For instance, in the chapter "Peace" of the teachers' guide *In the Global Classroom*, Pike and Selby begin with a debate of the Second World War, deterrence, disarmament, terrorism, and structural violence in society, but swiftly transition into discussion about "interpersonal peace" and "cooperative learning" to "foster conflict avoidance, mediation, and resolution skills."[31] The authors cite Mahatma Gandhi's quotation "there is no road to peace; peace is the road," to suggest that teachers should view peace less as a goal to strive for, but rather as "a process that should inform our relationships and behaviors."[32] In order to achieve "inner peacefulness," teaching strategies should be "aimed at harmonizing body, intellect, emotion, and intuition and helping students confront their concerns and fears."[33]

When conflict resolution and peace are taught as personal qualities rather than political topics of study, there is no quest to understand how nations and cultures have come into conflict, nor how they resolved those conflicts. In fact, the ethics of such conflicts and the ways in which they were resolved in different contexts is notably absent in these activities. Instead of opening children's minds to a world of human ethics, lessons in global ethics are designed with the expectation that children will internalize a nonconfrontational approach to problem solving.

Participation/Making a difference

"Students will develop a sense of efficacy and civic responsibility by identifying specific ways that they can make some contribution to the resolution of a global issue or challenge," report the authors of *Planning Curriculum in International Education*.[34] Learning about the issues in question is not the point of global ethics: children are expected to move from "engagement to reflection to action." However, not all global educators take the view that pupils must be involved in actions to address global issues and injustice. As one author observes, some proponents of global education were "less concerned with activism, *per se*, than they were with action that changes the perception of the individual."[35]

Hence, we can see that with teaching social justice and global issues the aim is often to change the values and attitudes of children rather than to solve "global" problems. Whatever actions children may take in the name of global justice, the action is instrumental to the goal of self-realization.[36]

This is why *participation* or *making a difference* can be promoted as a global value without due consideration to the content of what pupils are participating in, surely the prior question. While national education advocated for participation in a national democracy, global education encourages engagement with global ethics, each of which provides a guide for personal conduct and ambition. In this respect, global education appears to its advocates to provide an alternative moral framework, based upon a romantic assumption of inner goodness.

Global citizenship and interdependence

"But what do we mean by global citizenship?" asks Professor of Child Education Nel Noddings. Answering her own question, she replies, "This is not an easy question to answer, and the issues that arise as we try to answer it are difficult."[37] For Noddings, a global citizen has a *concern for* peace, worldwide economic and social justice, the health of our physical world, the preservation of well-loved places, the balance of diversity and unity, and the well-being of all of earth's inhabitants.[38] In essence, being a global citizen means having a certain attitude or ethos, an expression of "global" concerns, rather than membership of a community. This global citizen is an emotive individual, who can pick and choose which global issue they wish to care about. Yet in reality, these individual moral choices are simply reflecting back society's contemporary fears and concerns.

One teaching strategy for global citizenship that appears in a number of resources is to contrast the attitudes of a tourist, a traveler, and a global citizen. The tourist is just passing through a location. They do not try to interact with local people or sample the indigenous culture. The traveler is curious about the local people and their customs. They ask questions and seek interactions with their hosts. Finally, a global citizen feels at home in other cultures. They are used to communicating in another language and understand their hosts' customs. The global citizen returns frequently to places abroad. This analogy has been extended to the classroom in Wisconsin's *Planning Curriculum in International Education* (Box 5.3). Global citizens are seen here as those who have embraced global ethics and the skills to implement them. In other words, citizenship has been reinvented as an attitude, rather than the contribution of adults toward a politic. For this reason, it can be extended down to children.

The blurring of the lines between private and public realms has enabled global educators to cast children in the role of active citizens, whose private actions contribute to global processes. This has been called "deep citizenship" by some academics.[39] Here, children are coaxed into believing that by changing some aspect of their lifestyle they are effecting real change in the world. Global education tricks children into thinking that personal change and

BOX 5.3 TOURIST, TRAVELER, GLOBAL CITIZEN[40]

The Tourist Classroom	The Traveling Classroom	The Global Classroom
The tourist classroom samples food, hosts festivals, and studies about famous people of other countries.	The traveling classroom studies history, geography, economics, politics, and arts of another culture.	The global classroom studies a culture or issue in depth, focusing on complexities and contradictions.
Students focus on the unfamiliar, the exotic, and the differences between others and themselves.	The classroom invites in international teachers and cultural guests. The class travels, by fax, email, or short visits to the place itself.	Students work on collaborative projects with classrooms abroad and in other schools.
After a quick foray, they return to their regular curriculum.	The traveling classroom takes longer journeys, because questions lead to more questions, acquaintances bring more acquaintances.	The classroom exists in a school that practices skills for democracy and citizenship, including service learning.
The teacher is the tour guide.	Students are engaged in language study and know that achieving proficiency takes many years.	Students communicate through world languages they are learning, through the arts, and via new technologies.
	The teacher is a fellow explorer who brings learning skills and experiences to the shared journey.	The teacher, with students, participates in inquiry, dialogue and action. He creates opportunities for students to experience multiple perspectives.

Reprinted from *Planning Curriculum in International Education* (2002) with permission from the Wisconsin Department of Public Instruction, 125 S. Webster Street, Madison, WI 53703.

social change are the same thing. For example, *In the Global Classroom* recommends that children:

> [S]hould be helped to understand the connections that exist among all levels: for example, how their personal well-being is entwined with the economic and political decision making of governments around the world; how global environmental trends are influenced by human behavior and changes in local ecosystems. Local and global should be viewed not as opposite ends of a spectrum, but as overlapping spheres of activity in constant and dynamic interplay.[41]

But anyone who has tried to bring about some significant political change, such as the end of apartheid, civil rights for minorities or women's suffrage, knows that it takes a lot more than attitudinal adjustment to redirect the course of history.

With global thinking, interdependence exists at different levels, not just that of the community. While much of the world has been interdependent throughout the modern era, over the last couple of decades those in politics, the media, and academia have sold us the notion of growing interdependence through the prism of globalization. Global thinking means moving away from modernist assumptions about the importance of boundaries, both physical and theoretical. This holistic approach seeks, in turn, to challenge many of the dualisms arising from Cartesian thought, including nation/ex-nation, human/animal, masculine/feminine, and culture/nature, as well as Descartes' division of *res cognita* (mind) and *res extensa* (matter). These are replaced by a holistic philosophy of the world that perceives reality in a dynamic relational web, an unbroken wholeness.[42] For schools, this implies that teachers should teach pupils about these interconnections, rather than breaking the world and knowledge into discrete entities: geographical or political territories, subject disciplines, natural versus human, discrete histories, and cultures. However, as we see in the next chapter, education is impossible without drawing distinctions.

This postmodern philosophy has been embraced over decades by global activists and some progressives, but it is a viewpoint that has become more popular over recent years as the nation-state has become perceived as increasingly problematic. It also challenges many of the foundations upon which modern societies, including schools, were built. This includes the belief that humans are distinct from the natural world, something they have achieved through education and culture.

Sustainable development

In 2007, New Labour's Department for Children, Schools, and Families (formerly the Department for Education and Skills) launched its Sustainable Schools strategy with a view to making all schools "sustainable" by 2020. The strategy involves eight "doorways" to sustainability: food and drink, energy and water, travel and traffic, purchasing and waste, buildings and grounds, inclusion and participation, local well-being and the global dimension. Thus, a sustainable school is one that "procures healthy, ethically sourced food," showcases "energy efficiency, renewable energy use, and water conservation," promotes car sharing, public transportation, walking, and cycling to reduce traffic and pollution, embraces "reduce, reuse, and recycle" and local goods and services, is built and managed using "sustainable design principles" and "sustainable technologies," promotes community cohesion by providing "an inclusive, welcoming atmosphere that values everybody's participation and contribution," and encourages pupils to contribute to both local and global challenges.[43] In England, sustainability has become an all-pervasive ethos for schools, as well as an aim of national curriculum subjects.

The Reading International Solidarity Center (RISC) provides some sample outlines for sustainability assemblies. One example at primary level is *Food Shopping for Planet Earth* (Box 5.4), the aim of which is to "raise awareness of the impact our choice of food in the supermarket has on the planet."[44] In this activity, we can see how sustainable development, either explicitly or implicitly, promotes social justice and environmental values, through a concern for where, how, and by whom groceries were produced.

While it is educational for pupils to learn about where, how, and by whom the goods we consume are made, this is not the main purpose of sustainable development education. Rather, its inclusion in the curriculum of American and English schools is to promote the values implicit in the concept: that our current path of growth and progress is unsustainable. This means a revision of the very

BOX 5.4   FOOD SHOPPING FOR PLANET EARTH[45]

*P*lanet Earth is at the checkout today and wants your help in deciding what will be good for her. Person 1 asks the audience for a thumbs up or down for each item. Shopper at the checkout, Person 2, empties basket, holds up each item and says what it is and then packs it into the supermarket carrier bag:

- *Plantation banana*
- *Imported vegetables*
- *Biscuits with lots of packaging*
- *Factory farmed eggs*
- *Can of cola*

Shopper comments on trying to save time, effort, and money, but never thought about it from the earth's point of view . . . .[sic]

A week later

Planet Earth again asks audience to help in deciding what will be good for her. Shopper at the checkout again empties basket holds up each item and says what it is . . . and this time packs it into own canvas bag:

- *Fairtrade bananas*
- *Locally grown vegetables*
- *Biscuits with less packaging*
- *Free-range eggs*
- *Local apple juice*

What can we do?

Our lunch boxes and school dinners can make a difference— empty out an earth-friendly lunch box: local, organic, fair trade. Talk about earth-friendly dinners [sic].

Reprinted from *All You Need for a Sustainability Assembly* (2008) with permission from Reading International Solidarity Centre.

meaning of progress, as it celebrates development that is small-scale, local, rural, and labor intensive. In societies that are unable to offer citizens either a vision of social progress or widespread material progress, the message that our ambitions need to be curtailed by environmental limits seems rather too convenient.

This is perhaps best illustrated in response to the developing world, where sustainable development has had worrying outcomes. In *The Enemies of Progress: The Dangers of Sustainability*, Austin Williams shows how sustainable development "redefines the concept of progress and development to pretend that those in the developing world should be happy with less developed status."[46] Williams notes how some in the West have been aghast at the rapid industrialization and economic growth of China and India. "For devotees of sustainability, it's simply common sense that such rapid growth and accompanying rise in aspiration and expectation are far too unsustainable. The tipping point is being reached, we are told and China and India could be on the verge of pushing things over the edge," writes Williams.[47] Sustainable development education promotes rural microdevelopment, as has been encouraged in many African countries by numerous nongovernmental development organizations (often the same ones writing the curriculum materials on development for schools). In other words, this is development without industrialization, development without economic growth. Williams finds "a patronizing imposition of sustainability on aspiring economies is simply ethical colonialism designed to keep them in their place."[48]

What is missed in contemporary environmental and sustainability education is a critical examination of the premises upon which they stand. Fundamental to this ideology is the notion that resources are finite. This perspective fails to acknowledge that natural materials only become resources through human ingenuity, and that history shows that humanity has managed to grow its stock of natural resources to keep pace with advancing industrialization and population growth. For instance, nuclear, solar, wind, or geothermal power were once the stuff of pipedreams: now they all contribute to our energy needs. On a day to day basis, we do still depend upon natural goods, but by definition, very little of human activity is natural. It is our ability to transcend the limits of natural resources which contributes to our humanity. It is therefore disturbing that, with its environmentally centered approach, sustainable development displaces furthering humanity as the purpose of action.

Human rights

Programs in global education include a reverence for human rights, as presented in the UN Universal Declaration on Human Rights, and a related disdain for nationally defined rights. A 2001 survey of US states found that forty per cent included mandates, standards, guidelines or proficiencies for human rights education.[49] Here, we use an activity about child labor from TeachUNICEF as an example of human rights education: "The Impact of Child Labor" for grades 6–8 (Box 5.5). The activity tells the story of teenager working in a restaurant at a Palestinian camp in Jordan.

The materials gathered by UNICEF clearly have educative potential. It is important for American and English pupils to learn that in some countries around the world the lives of children are very different from theirs, and they should learn about the conditions which deprive children of education and force them into labor. Nevertheless, they should also learn that because of these differences one cannot immediately impose Western standards of rights and childrearing, which is what the UNICEF lessons do. The 1948 Universal Declaration of Human Rights was produced in Geneva, based on Western ideals. It is not uncommon for teenagers in developing countries to support families, who might otherwise go without basic necessities. Would it be better if these young people went to school? Sure. But this is an unrealistic expectation of families in less developed countries, who live close to the poverty line. Only by raising the standard of living across the country, which necessitates widespread economic growth, will parents achieve a better social and economic position so that they are no longer dependent upon their children for income. Unfortunately, UNICEF is not interested in exploring alternate avenues for Ali's family. Rather, in the follow-up lesson, pupils are introduced to UNICEF's Child Protection policy and the work undertaken in its name.

This lesson is designed not so that pupils understand that in other countries different ethical norms arise from different socioeconomic conditions and cultural practices, but to imply that Western ethical

BOX 5.5 ALI'S STORY: THE IMPACT OF CHILD LABOR[50]

Lesson 1: Child's Work (extract)

Opening Activity: Students interview each other about the work they do inside and outside of the home.

Students watch Ali's Video about a teenager working at a restaurant in a Palestinian camp in Jordon. They then read Ali's Story:

> *Everyday Ali works at a falafel restaurant. He fries chick-pea patties, makes sandwiches, and cleans up. He works 8 hours a day during the school year and 12 hours a day during his summer break. While Ali works, he can see his friends laughing as they kick a soccer ball on the dusty streets. He wants to join them, but cannot. Ali knows that he must work to help his family make ends meet, because severe back and eyesight problems prevent his father from working.*

Students discuss the following questions:

- *What skills do you think Ali has?*
- *Why does Ali work?*
- *How might his family be affected if he did not work?*
- *What worries Ali about working?*
- *Why do you think Ali says he is hopeful about his future?*

Lesson 2: Putting an End to All Work and No Play (extract)

Opening Activity: Students complete a Time Chart to illustrate Ali's daily activities and make comparisons to their own lives.
Students read about UNICEF's Child Protection policy[51]
Volunteers describe in their own words acceptable forms of child's work and unacceptable forms of child labor.

(Continued)

Ask the students: Based on Ali's time chart, do you think that he is involved in an unacceptable form of child labor?

Students brainstorm what other kinds of programs could be created to help working children.

Students read 'UNICEF at Work: Ending Child Labor' (describing different UNICEF programs on child labor).

Assessing solutions: Students are asked to consider the relationships between poverty, education, and child labor and to consider what kind of programs would be most helpful to Ali and children like him.

Reproduced from *Ali's Story: The Impact of Child Labor* with permission from TeachUNICEF.

standards are superior to those of Jordan and show that we can devise "programs" that will "help" children like Ali. In other words, it establishes an ethical divide between the civilized "here" and the apparently less civilized developing "there": a lesson that could be used to educate children about contrasting ethics and the reasons for these standards ends up uncritically reinforcing Western norms.

Conclusion: Global ethics—Not so ethical after all

Global ethics in the Anglo-American curriculum are **antieducational** because they replace academic knowledge with personal reflection as the goal of learning. While an understanding of ethics is an important part of education, knowledge, as any good teacher will tell you, is the path to understanding, including in the area of morality. Having said this, in some classrooms today, pupils often learn knowledge in pursuit of global ethics. This may be partly because those teaching global education are more motivated by the rationale of global ethics than they are to teach subjects. Teaching necessitates communication, and when teachers are passionate about learning, they inspire children to do likewise. But this does not hide the fact that global education rejects theoretical knowledge as the basis for education, and thus the knowledge learned in pursuit of global ethics will lack a conceptual framework of understanding. It will just be lots of bits of knowledge without a framework through which pupils can see how the knowledge fits together.

Further, learning about global ethics is not the same thing as an education in ethical thought. Learning about morality involves the study of an array of human problems in multifarious cultural, geographical, political, or historical contexts. In the humanities, pupils should "confront a wider and more disturbing diversity of opinion" than they get in everyday life.[52] The idea is to challenge pupils so that they can see different points of view and become aware of the complexity of moral problems. Through an exploration of the human condition, children will begin to develop their own moral compass to help them understand the logic behind different ethical standpoints, a prerequisite for political thought and participation. In contrast, with global education the purpose is not to explore ethics but rather to internalize a standpoint that discourages engaging with moral debate and making judgments. Such an approach can only undermine the intellectual development and autonomy of children, as well as that of communities.

In this way, global ethics are also **antidemocratic**. The very functioning of liberal democracies is predicated upon autonomous subjects, who, in the words of Jefferson, "armed with knowledge and literature" are capable of providing a check on the rule of leaders. In democracies, citizens play a public role in defining the values upon which society will be based, a vision of where it is heading, and also how to respond to domestic and international events. With global ethics this process is inversed. Each of the global ethics listed in this chapter in some way dictates how children should engage in global issues. In place of an active moral subject, who mediates change through an expression of personal and collective interests, the global individual is shaped by "global forces" beyond their control. "When we engage 'globally' we engage with less social connection, with less social mediation, making our actions less strategic or instrumental, less clearly goal-orientated," notes Chandler, in his critique of human rights and foreign policy.[53] Therefore, when politics is globalized it becomes increasingly abstract and distant. Where global ethics blurs the boundaries of the private and public realms this implies the demise of the latter, which means the demise of politics. Because global ethics rejects the public realm in favor of personal actions it lacks a theory of social change, and hence a conception of history and social progress. Children are being disingenuously coaxed into believing that by tweaking their lifestyle they are magically redirecting "global processes," the outcome of which is more likely to be political disillusionment than engagement.

Global ethics are also **a-cultural**, because they lack a social basis upon which people could be united. In fact, global ethics are premised upon a rejection of culturally defined communities, bound together by some common beliefs and interests. Without a cultural context through which morality gains meaning, global ethics become abstract standards, which surely means that they are not really ethics at all, since our sense of what is good and bad can only exist in relation to a social context. Teaching children that they should hold a global perspective is another way of saying that they should not define their outlook by that which they hold in common with others. This is why Nodding wants to replace "interest" with "concern" in her conception of global citizenship. Expressing interests means identifying something in common with other people and necessitates an active engagement with the outside world in order to bring about some meaningful change; expressing a concern or values is an individual act and does not necessarily mean external engagement. Children are encouraged to show a concern for global issues and do their own bit. However, because these are personal acts lacking attachment to a notion of social progress, any "external engagement or attachment," (such as empathy) "is instrumental to the internal effect."[54] The ends are therefore therapeutic: not orientated outward to the world, but focused inward, on the self.

Global activists and educators might respond by arguing that global citizens are united through their identification with global ethics and their collective endeavors to address global issues. But most global issues are external to the child's society and so lack a public focus for understanding.[55] Subscribing to global ethics demands only individual attitudes and actions as determined by global forces, from which human agency is removed. This can be contrasted with the way American multicultural education in the 1970s and 1980s developed in response to minority struggles for equal representation in society. This was a movement with a political base and a constituency demanding that different cultures be represented in American society. In other words, it was about "us." In contrast, global education seeks meaning for individuals not in relation to their own communities or society, but through an "Other."[56]

Notes

1 Morris (1979).

2 Wisconsin Department of Public Instruction, "Framework for International Education Lesson Design," handout provided at teacher training event on international education, New Jersey, 2004.

3 Pigozzi (2006) p. 3.

4 Crews (1989) p. 28.

5 Oxfam (2006) p. 7.

6 Nolan (1998) p. 143.

7 Ecclestone and Hayes (2009).

8 Nolan (1998).

9 Pike and Selby (1988) pp. 120–21.

10 Ibid. p. 147.

11 Department for Education and Skills (2005) p. 13.

12 O'Neil, B., "Turning Immigration into a Tool of Social Engineering," *Spiked-Online*, 2010. Accessed: http://www.spiked-online.com/index.php/site/article/8335/

13 Ibid.

14 Tye (1991) p. 5.

15 Reminers, F., "Preparing Students for the Flat World," *Education Week*, 28(7), pp. 24–5, 2008.

16 Furedi, F., "The Truth About Tolerance," *Spiked-online*, 29 December 2010. Accessed: http://www.spiked-online.com/index.php/site/reviewofbooks_article/10034/

17 Nolan (1998) p. 147.

18 Furedi (2011).

19 Ibid. p. 81.

20 Burack (2003) p. 53.

21 Wisconsin Department of Public Instruction (2002) p. 23.

22   Furedi (2009) p. 177.

23   Reading International Solidarity Center, *Growing Bananas: A Simulation about Fair Trade for KS 2-3*, 2005. p. 1.

24   Development Education Association (2004) p. 24.

25   Source: Oxfam website, cited in Development Education Association (2004) p. 24.

26   Department for Education and Skills (2005) p. 13.

27   Pike and Selby (2000) p. 130.

28   National Association for International Schools, "Challenge 20/20 Video," 2007. Accessed: http://www.nais.org/global/movie. cfm?ItemNumber=149859

29   Wisconsin Department of Public Instruction (2002) p. 8.

30   Pike and Selby (2000) p. 42.

31   Ibid. p. 54.

32   Ibid. p. 55.

33   Ibid. p. 55.

34   Wisconsin Department of Public Instruction (2002) p. 34.

35   Gaudelli (2003) p. 23.

36   Eccelstone and Hayes (2009) p. 124.

37   Noddings (2005) p. 1.

38   Ibid. p. 4.

39   Machon and Walkington (2001).

40   Wisconsin Department of Public Instruction (2002) p. 39.

41   Pike and Selby (2000) p. 13.

42   Bohm, 1983, cited by Selby (2000) p. 89.

43   Department for Children, Schools and Families, "Sustainable Schools for Pupils, Communities and the Environment: The Eight Doorways to Sustainability," 2007. Accessed: http://www.teachernet.gov.uk/ sustainableschools

44   RISC (2008) *All you Need for a Sustainability Assembly*. Reading International Solidarity Center, p. 2.

45   Ibid. pp. 2–3.

46   Williams (2008) p. 109.

47   Ibid. p. 88.

48   Ibid. p. 109.

49 Banks (2002).

50 UNICEF, "Ali's Story: The Impact of Child Labor, lesson 1 & 2," 2010. Accessed: *http://teachunicef.org/explore/topic/child-labor*

51 UNICEF, "Child Protection Information Sheet: Child Labor," 2006 Accessed: *http://www.unicef.org/protection/files/Child_Labour.pdf*

52 Kronman (2007).

53 Chandler (2009) p. 208.

54 Ecclestone and Hayes (2009) p. 124.

55 Heilman (2009) p. 32.

56 Ibid. p. 33.

6

The essential boundaries for learning about the world

Thus far, we have seen that in the twenty-first century the term "global" has been used to imply a lack of specificity, uncertainty, distance, intangibility, and a lack of rootedness to communities. In the context of education, this is problematic because it generates uncertainty about what to teach and why we should teach it. This chapter will examine the boundaries that are essential for education to take place, in whichever context.

There are two ways in which education needs to be bounded. First, in order to clarify the meaning of education we need to understand how the nature of education is different from other human endeavors. We need to know what is distinctive about education since the moral worth of something derives from its unique qualities. Or, to put it another way, boundaries are a precondition for meaningfulness.[1] When education becomes combined with other activities like social reform or vocational training, its inherent quality is undermined and the meaning of education becomes confused.

Second, education needs to be bounded by communities of adults including teachers, administrators, parents, subject specialists, and other like-minded adults. Education is more likely to be successful in a community of adults who share some basic assumptions about the knowledge and values we want to pass on to our children. This is because what is taught in schools, and the practice of education, is intimately tied to notions of who we are and what we value.[2] These communities do not have to be geographically bounded nor necessarily bounded by a political territory, although oftentimes they are. Nevertheless, in clarifying what it is they value, their beliefs, they are making a distinction between themselves and people who hold other beliefs. Such a moral framework derived from a community is what global education is lacking.

The boundary between education and social/individual reform

The practice of making distinctions is fundamental to the very process of education. Only through identifying boundaries, can people begin to see order and coherence where previously they saw disorder and disarray. Imagine an infant who stands and looks out onto a rural landscape and sees different shapes, colors, textures, and movement. How can they even begin to comprehend this array of information? The answer is, only through social constructs such as plant, animal, human, hill, field, farming, sky, sun, wind, road, school, house, farm, and so forth. Each of these concepts or practices must be established in the child's mind through a process of education, distinguishing each category from others.

Making distinctions is therefore the very basis of knowledge.[3] In the early part of the twentieth century, Durkheim noted that distinctions of ideas become knowledge when they are organized into a system or are placed in connection with one another. Drawing distinctions is important at postgraduate level as well as in elementary education, but to very different degrees of abstraction. The objective in both instances, in fact the aim of education, is to achieve clarity of understanding; to make sense of something where before there was confusion. While individuals occasionally gain new insights which further our understanding of the world, they only achieve this through a system of distinctions (knowledge) already in place in society. Passing on the cumulative knowledge of mankind to children is, therefore, the process of education.

So how do we distinguish education from political action, training, saving the environment, narrowing the skills gap, inclusion, achieving social justice or other extrinsic aims that are included under the heading of global education? We have already acknowledged above that education is tied to a vision of who we are and what we stand for; hence, it is connected to our beliefs and political ideas. Nevertheless, just because we aim to pass on our values to children through education does not mean that we have turned education into a political activity. What we choose to teach, and how we teach it, is informed by our perspective on the world, but decisions about the curriculum must proceed on educational rather than political or economic grounds. It is a question of the purpose of teaching. If the aim of a lesson is to instill an attitude of tolerance or empathy in children or to change their consumption habits in order to reduce carbon emissions, then this is a therapeutic or political activity—not an educational one.

Stanley Fish has written a book about the line between education and political activism in higher education. In *Save the World on Your Own Time,* he notes that universities and colleges can legitimately undertake two tasks:

1) Introduce students to bodies of knowledge and traditions of inquiry they didn't know much about before; and 2) equip those same students with the analytical skills – of argument, statistical modeling, laboratory procedure – that will enable them to move confidently within those traditions and to engage in independent research after a course is over.[4]

Now, there is an important difference between schools and higher education: schools teach children and universities instruct young adults (more on this boundary below). This matters because children do not have the knowledge and experience to determine their own values and beliefs, although they are certainly beginning to form ideas about them. They have an immature moral compass, so children need adults to guide them. Thus, schools have a somewhat different task than institutions of higher education. But Fish's account is useful because he identifies the line between educational and political activities in the classroom, at whichever level. What matters is not necessarily the topic under investigation, but how it is approached. Political topics can be discussed, but the task of the educator is to "academicize" the issues, suggests Fish. This means that the question or topic is turned into an object of study rather than a tool for changing behavior, attitudes, or the world: "To academicize a topic is to detach it from the context of its real world urgency, where there is a vote to be taken or an agenda to be embraced, and insert it into a context of academic urgency, where there is an account to be offered or an analysis to be performed."[5] In other words, an educational classroom is one in which issues are studied in order to understand the problem better: what is at stake, and how people are responding to it. Activism ensues the minute a teacher starts to proselytize or moralize to their charges. How does a teacher know when they are academicizing? In Fish's view "Just apply a simple test: am I asking my students to produce or assess an account of a vexed political issue, or am I asking my students to pronounce on the issue?"[6]

When it comes to passing on values and beliefs to children, it is also necessary to distinguish between those values and ideas that are held by the community or society at large and attempts to change society through influencing the values and attitudes of children. Thus, Furedi differentiates between socialization *into* the norms and values of a society, the process of social renewal, and social engineering which seeks to *challenge* and *alter* those norms and values.[7] As an "instigator" of global change,[8] global education clearly comes into the latter category. Its primary goal is to change the values, attitudes, and behavior of children, who in turn are expected to influence the behavior and attitudes of their parents. This Furedi calls "socialization in reverse"—children being used to "educate" their parents. Clearly, the aspirations of global educators are for social and political change, rather than education specifically. As such the proper place for their efforts is the political realm, not schools.

The boundary between public and private

Education has become increasingly confused with politics only because the line between the public and private realms in society has also become blurred. This is largely due to the decline of politics as a means to further our interests and make sense of our lives. The public sphere refers to those activities that take place in public view: politics, work, school, community, public organizations, and so forth, otherwise known as civil society. In contrast, the private realm takes place away from the eye of the public: home, personal consumption, private consciousness, and personal relations. This boundary has historically been considered an essential part of liberal democracy because individual autonomy and active engagement in the public realm are dependent upon a private space into which one can withdraw and reflect upon one's public role.[9]

The role of schools and colleges in liberal democracies has generally been a public one: to pass on the knowledge and cultural traditions held in common by society. In England, being a nation of long-standing traditions and knowledge, the content of the curriculum—at least, until recent decades—reflected its traditions and disciplinary knowledge. Before it was mandated by the New Labour government in 2000, most schools did not teach citizenship as a subject. With a strong liberal tradition and national identity, it was generally not viewed as a necessity. Nevertheless, the curriculum was overtly national in orientation with subjects such as English and history communicating a sense of national identity. As with many nations, one of the primary functions of schools was to educate children in the knowledge and skills that were needed to participate in society as adults: economically, politically, and socially.

With the United States being a relatively new nation of people from different traditions, things are somewhat different. Lacking deeply rooted traditions, schooling children in the ideals of the Republic was even more essential to social renewal. Thomas Jefferson, John Adams, James Madison, Benjamin Franklin, and other founders were all worried that the Republic would survive. They viewed common schooling in language, knowledge, and American ideals as essential for this task. This sentiment was captured in an 1845 address to the legislature by Governor Silas Wright:

> On the careful cultivation in our schools, of the minds of the young, the entire success or the absolute failure of the great experiment of self government is wholly dependent; and unless that cultivation is increased, and made more effective that it has yet been, the conviction is solemnly impressed by the signs of the times, that the American Union, now the asylum of the oppressed

and 'the home of the free,' will ere long share the melancholy fate of every former attempt of self government. That Union is and must be sustained by the moral and intellectual powers of the community, and every other power is wholly ineffectual. Physical force may generate hatred, fear and repulsion; but can never produce Union. The only salvation for the republic is to be sought for in our schools.[10]

Governor Wright was wrong that the entire success or failure of the Republic was dependent upon schooling. It is in the political realm where such matters are determined. Nevertheless, Wright implicitly understood that educating each generation in the "moral and intellectual powers of the community" was a necessary part of sustaining the community.

Over recent decades, the significance of the public realm has changed as participation in political life has declined and fewer citizens view their lives as contributing to the collective well being and improvement of the nation. Instead, they are *Bowling Alone*, argues Robert Putnam.[11] This does not mean that people don't want to make a difference to society, but that many of the institutions that used to channel people's aspirations for social betterment (including political parties and trade unions) are today rarely able to carry out this function to the same degree. Instead, people are more likely to volunteer locally or contribute to nonprofits like Peace Corps.

Today, the public realm has become less political. People are more likely to define themselves through their job, their ethnic culture, their favorite sports team, religion, music, through parenting or contributing to a charitable cause. When politics is held in low esteem and appears unable to offer the potential to change our lives for the better, we search for other forms of identity.[12] As the decline of the public realm has elevated the importance of the personal sphere, it could be argued that the personal has indeed become political: what we consume, the brand of clothes we wear, which laundry detergent we use, the size of our carbon footprint, whether we demonstrate empathy for others . . . all of these personal actions and values have taken on added meaning, as they have become exposed to public scrutiny. The expression "Think Global, Act Local" sums up the contemporary belief that personal actions have wider, direct political significance.

The elevation of the importance of personal actions misunderstands how political change takes place, and is one of the main drivers behind the confusion between education and politics. Erosion of belief in the ideals of America has caused a commensurate shift in schools. According to E. D. Hirsch, "By the 1950s they [schools] no longer conceived their chief mission to create educated citizens who shared a sense of public commitment and community."[13] Here, Hirsch was referring to growing influence of the progressive education movement, which had become the dominant approach in education colleges by this time. In elevating individual development over social and cultural aims, progressives led the teaching profession down the path toward a therapeutic or private conception of education.

Decades later, the conflation of the private and public realms is even more clearly expressed by global education. For instance, the idea of global citizenship offers a privatized notion of citizenship for which academic education is not necessary. This is because it demands that children make a connection between their personal lives and "global processes." With global citizenship the rationale for learning is to understand how events are directly relevant to you and to work out how you can "make a difference." Here, the purpose of education is to make meaning for your life (as an individual), rather than learning about the knowledge and ideas accumulated by generations. In essence, the privatized conception of education provides its advocates with a rationale for helping children to feel good about themselves, but it lacks a rationale for educating them.

The boundary between children and adults

The boundary between adults and children parallels the boundary between the public and the private realm. This is because children, as immature and undeveloped beings, are not yet able to make a valid contribution to the political realm. By the very nature of childhood, children should be protected from the responsibilities and pressures of adulthood.

Decades ago, Hannah Arendt alerted the world to the pernicious effects of turning schools into institutions with instrumental ends. She cautioned that a certain "destruction of the real living space occurs whenever the attempt is made to turn children themselves into a kind of world."[14] Yet this is precisely what global education seeks to do. It imports problems from the outside world into schools, not to study them, but to use them as a means to transmit values and skills to children. Whether it is the skills gap, environmental crisis, racial intolerance, inequality, the declining meaning of citizenship, or human rights, global education is seeking to solve problems from the adult public sphere by displacing them into the classroom. This is unfair to both teachers and children. To expect school to address political, economic, and social problems can only interfere with the job of teaching. And, asking children *really* to participate in solving real world problems (as opposed to mimicking participation) is to not treat them as children at all.

For education to be successful, its institutions need a degree of separation from the real world. Children need "a place of security where they can grow."[15] This does not mean that they ignore the real world: that is the object of their study, after all. However, for teachers to be able to teach and children to learn, they need to be sheltered from the pressures of the real world, including market forces and political problems. Within the confines of the school walls, teachers can focus on teaching knowledge and skills, and together teachers and children can explore ideas and topics without responsibility for solving problems in the outside world or meeting government-imposed targets. It is with the provision of this space that teachers can freely introduce children to Hamlet, foreign languages, distant countries and cultures, Chopin, molecular biology, ancient civilizations, and revolutions, as well as political and economic theories and problems. Armed with this knowledge and literature, they will be well prepared to assume the responsibilities of adulthood, including political responsibility, when they finish school.

Conversely, in the act of bounding a private realm, for both education and a personal space for adults, it becomes clearer where adult responsibilities lie: solving political, social, economic, and environmental problems. In other words, a revitalized private realm is connected to a rekindled political life. As we will see below, successful education depends upon a vibrant public community.

The boundary between theoretical and everyday knowledge

From the above discussion, we know that education takes place through the acquisition of knowledge. Yet, this is not just any kind of knowledge. Intuitively, we know that some knowledge is more important than other knowledge. Almost everybody pokes fun at degrees in golf studies or car sales. Global education emphasizes knowledge of other cultures, foreign language skills, the environment, issues of global concern, and problem solving, at the expense of academic knowledge. It is asserted that these areas of knowledge are more relevant to the needs of citizens in a global world in which knowledge and information are continually being updated. Advocates of global education often reject subject disciplines because they are focused on the past (and present) as well as their association with national ruling elites; even when global education includes subjects such as foreign languages, history, and geography its aims are to teach global values and global skills rather than disciplinary knowledge. So does it matter if pupils study subject disciplines or global issues and global culture?

The significant boundary to draw here is between everyday knowledge and theoretical knowledge.[16] Everyday knowledge refers to the knowledge that we gain through personal experiences and encounters. While we may reflect upon the knowledge we acquire in our daily lives, it will always be limited to our subjective viewpoint and limited experiences. In contrast, theoretical knowledge is obtained by abstracting from one particular context and placing ideas in relation to each other. This distinction is derived from Durkheim's distinction between "sacred" and "profane" orders of meaning.[17] The "profane" refers to people's everyday lives in which concerns are practical, immediate, and particular to their circumstances, while the "sacred" world of religion is invented, abstract, and collective. For Durkheim, the collective representations of the sacred world do not originate in individual minds, but rather from communities. Hence, it is sociality that gives knowledge its objective quality.

This model was advanced by Basil Bernstein's conception of horizontal and vertical knowledge. Horizontal knowledge is akin to the everyday realm, in that it is context-dependent and unstructured, while vertical knowledge is hierarchical and accessible only via symbolic structures and specific principles. In other words, vertical or theoretical knowledge is abstract and can only be accessed through systems of concepts and ideas, while horizontal knowledge is context-dependent. In modern times, theoretical knowledge has been organized into subject disciplines.

Both everyday and theoretical knowledge have their place in education. Often, teachers will make connections between abstract knowledge and concrete examples to facilitate learning. Schools may also choose to offer some lessons in more practical endeavors such as computing, design and technology, or healthcare. Nevertheless, what is unique to education as a formal setting is the teaching of theoretical or academic knowledge. What is different about theoretical knowledge is that it takes pupils beyond their everyday lives and introduces them to different worlds and experiences. This includes learning about people in a foreign country, their culture, their language, their history, their economic and political system, as well as the theories and ideas that give disciplines their internal coherence. Theoretical knowledge is also more powerful than everyday knowledge because of its explanatory power and also its practical application—think of all the social benefits derived from advances in science.

Theoretical knowledge is how we arrive at an understanding of how objects are related to each other, from which we can identify patterns of behavior and theories about phenomena. The leap from everyday to theoretical knowledge enables us to perceive relations between objects and ideas that are not intuitively apparent from personal experiences. We do this by manipulating representations of objects and ideas in our heads. Moreover, it is because thought occurs at the abstract or theoretical level, in detachment from empirical connections tied to specific contexts, which allows "one to bind together things which sensations leave apart."[18] Taking distance from objects and data also enables one to add new propositions, ad infinitum, extending our collective knowledge. Finally, without ties to everyday problems, we are better able to project toward somewhere we deem more desirable.[19]

This last point raises another question about global education. It shows us that it is theoretical knowledge, not every-day experiences, that provide us with the insight and understanding from which we are well placed to project into the future with informed judgment. Without academic knowledge, "futures thinking" will be an immature thought at best. Further, if education is reduced to personal and everyday knowledge, then how can pupils possibly obtain genuine perspectives that are different from their own? In the end, it is theoretical knowledge that adds perspective to one's experience and knowledge, not global education.

The boundary between mind and reality

The boundary between mind and reality is again important for helping us to make sense of the meaning of education. This boundary has become blurred in global education, with its aim of changing reality through the minds of children. This is particularly evident in the teaching of global ethics. For example, we saw in Chapter 5 that when global educators teach about peace and conflict resolution they do not treat these problems as needing a political resolution in the real world, but rather as "a process that should inform our relationships and behaviors." [20] In this and other examples, the lesson moves between the real world and the personal attitudes and values of children as if conflicts around the world are connected to the inner lives of children. Thus, *In the Global Classroom* encourages teachers to aim for interpersonal peace and inner peacefulness by helping pupils confront their concerns and fear.[21]

The conflation of reality and our knowledge of that reality stems from the theory of social constructivism. This theory helps us to understand that knowledge is socially contextual: that it is created in a given social and cultural context (as with Durkheim's notion of sacred knowledge). However, some social constructionists take this theory further, asserting that all reality is a social construct. Here, the relationship between object and representations of objects has been inverted: reality itself is all in the mind. This is how global educators arrive at the conclusion that changing children's attitudes and values about the world is the same thing as changing the world.

If it were true that there is no reality outside of how we think about it, this would mean that there is no knowledge of the world separate from people's lived experiences and there is no truth to uncover. But without a relationship to truth, knowledge loses its meaning. It becomes all a matter of opinion and perspective, and there are no criteria for distinguishing between right and wrong history, or better and worse literature. On the other hand, if there is a reality independent from our minds, then we must be able to know it, to a greater or lesser extent, and there are criteria by which we decide which knowledge and ideas are more accurate than others. The objectivity of truth claims are dependent upon their external validity (how well concepts and theories deal with the objects they are representing), their internal consistency or logic, and support from a community of experts.[22] As Johan Muller notes, although all inferences are formally the same "they are not all equally commendable."[23] They differ in terms of "consistency, explanatory power, fecundity, comprehensiveness and simplicity" as well as coherence and "epistemic gain."[24]

This is not to be blind to the social context in which knowledge is produced. We have already noted that theoretical knowledge is social and therefore culturally biased. But as one abstracts from a given social context and is able to make connections with different contexts, knowledge becomes objective—it transcends the historical and cultural conditions of its generation. Michael Young calls this a social realist approach to knowledge.

The purpose of education is to comprehend reality, and for that to happen we need to recognize our separation from the real world. Education is the process of making sense of reality in our minds. This is the challenging task educators have taken on-board. The authority of teachers and scholars, suggests Bernard Williams, depends upon the truthfulness of their claims: "Do the best you can to acquire true beliefs, and what you say reveals what you believe."[25] Pedagogues need to understand the world, and they have to find a way to communicate this to children and young adults.

The boundary between teaching and learning

If global educators display uncertainty toward academic Knowledge (with a capital "K") then they are more inclined towards child-centered learning than adult-centered teaching. Because they refrain from identifying a body of knowledge worthy of passing on to children, advocates of global education are ambivalent about the role of the teacher. For this reason, global educators promote a progressive philosophy that views education as coming from the child rather than the adult. In this approach, education is seen as a natural process of unfolding the child's inner abilities through discovery learning. Rather than imposing adult knowledge on children, progressive educators aim for children to find their own path to knowledge, skills, and values (although they often surreptitiously control teaching materials in order to communicate desired values and skills). Here, they are said to be constructing their own knowledge, skills, and values; constructing their own identity, even. Nevertheless, given that lessons are frequently constructed with their global ethics in mind, it is evident that global educators aim to play a significant part in this process of forming the child's identity.

The social constructivist, progressive, and market-based approaches to education have all become more popular with the decline of national culture and political leadership. Western societies have grown more ambivalent about what to teach and the role of the teacher. Global education encompasses the trend away from teaching and towards learning, which has been identified by several authors.[26] Ecclestone and Hayes assert that developments in the UK have gone further still, with learning being replaced with "feeling good about yourself:" "From education to learning, from learning to learning to learn, and from learning to learn to learning to feel and respond "appropriately," the collapse of belief in human potential is palpable."[27]

But teaching and learning are not the same thing. Where teachers have replaced teaching with learning, the education of children is at stake and often it is the "lower-ability" pupils who suffer most. In a study of mathematics teaching in the UK, Paul Dowling found that while "higher-ability" pupils were taught theoretical mathematics classes for lower-ability children focused on problems that modeled everyday examples.[28] The study concluded that lower-ability pupils were effectively excluded from learning mathematical relationships and theorems that would have helped them better understand the problems they were studying. Muller reports: "In substituting procedure for discourse, constructivism obscures the interconnected and generalized nature of school mathematics and precludes the induction of students into the discipline."[29]

Whether children learn knowledge, skills, and values by themselves or from adults, these are social goods that originate in our
society. In essence, they have come from us, not from the child.
Is it not the role of adults in society to decide which knowledge,
skills, and values children should learn? And, is it not the job and
responsibility of teachers to communicate knowledge, values, and
skills to their charges? This is teaching. Without it, children won't
learn much about the world.

The boundary between
subject disciplines

It is an unfortunate, though not unconnected, irony that the global
era has been characterized as a "knowledge society" at the same
time as theoretical knowledge has become less valued. The reason
for this contradiction is the way in which the term is used. When
knowledge becomes global, it is opened up to alternative meanings
and consequently it loses its special status. While in recent decades
subject knowledge has often been portrayed as conservative and
elitist, other types of knowledge have been celebrated. In addition
to personal or everyday knowledge, hybrid knowledge as applied
to solving problems has become revered. This applied knowledge
is that which is being celebrated in the idea of a knowledge society.
Some have even argued that problem solving equates to a new mode
of knowledge production that is transdisciplinary, transinstitu-
tional, and collaborative.[30]

Despite the high-pitched rhetoric, problem solving is not a
new form of knowledge, even if it can lead to new solutions and
provide new insights for disciplines. The elevated status of hybrid
knowledge and problem solving has more to do the prominence
of the economic rationale for education in our globalized society,
and the intrusion of business practices into schools. "Knowledge"
in the world of business is different from an academic setting. The
survival of companies does depend upon their ability to innovate
and stay current with respect to the latest technology, ideas, and
market conditions. But this type of knowledge is entirely different
from disciplinary knowledge. In the market place, what count
is providing desirable products and services, as well as solving

problems, like the need for lower carbon-emitting energy sources. While disciplinary knowledge can and should be put to social uses, it also has its own purpose.

Disciplinary knowledge is different from applied knowledge because most disciplines are defined by the object of their study. Although disciplines sometimes overlap, each has its own unique approach to knowledge, evidenced by hierarchical concepts and structures of knowledge. Although politics and economics are related disciplines, someone trained in one of them cannot easily jump into the other. It can also be a good thing to be trained in more than one related discipline (students at Oxford and other universities can be inducted in politics, philosophy, and economics). With such a background, the connections between different disciplines can facilitate comprehension of related developments in the real world. Nevertheless, such an approach does not detract from the uniqueness of each discipline. It is this specialism in a field of knowledge that enables scholars to push the frontiers of knowledge and understanding.

What those who advocate the teaching of problem solving and other skills of the global marketplace miss is that the cognitive abilities and skills they desire are developed through disciplinary training. "We learn higher-order modeling skills in specific discourses first. Genericity consists in generalizing the skill to analogous situations," noted Muller.[31] Thus, we reject the boundary between subject disciplines at our peril. To do so would cost us both the knowledge developed by specialists in the field and the skills necessary to apply this knowledge in the real world. It is far better to cultivate knowledge by communities of specialists who are then capable of training the next generation to surpass their insights.

The boundary between education and training

In both the English and American instances, it is clear that the convergence of academic and vocational education has harmed both practices.[32] A curriculum focused on generic "skills," or competencies as divorced from knowledge, offers neither an education nor training for jobs. Instead, children are asked to fulfill mundane tasks and activities or receive instruction in how to manage their personal lives and psychological well being.[33] This is neither education nor training. Training for the flexibility of the market or learning to learn has no inner qualities to pass on to children. Rather, they resemble platitudes that are reactive to instrumental demands.[34] In England, the expansion of competence-based vocational qualifications in schools has wrested responsibility for qualifications and accreditation away from the communities of professionals who are best-placed to train young adults, and placed it in the hands of government and quasigovernmental bodies.

As has already been stated, the quality of an activity depends upon its uniqueness. Education and vocational training are different types of activities utilizing different skills sets. They place different demands upon an individual and require different techniques of induction, which depend upon adults who have specialized knowledge and skills. For instance, academic education cannot be measured by precise outcomes. The process of education is open ended because we cannot always anticipate what will be learned from a course of study. Thankfully, the human mind is not that predictable. In contrast, training for a given job means demonstrating that certain tasks can be performed. While it is true that in some professions creativity and innovation are highly desirable qualities, most employees in most jobs will be performing known tasks most of the time, and training therefore involves learning the skills and knowledge needed to perform the job at hand. The disparate nature of education and training is why it is important to place a boundary between them. This may also mean that they are better off in different institutional settings.

Above, we emphasized the importance of insularity for academic disciplines. We have also noted that acquisition of theoretical knowledge develops higher-level cognitive abilities that can be applied in analogous situations.[35] This is one way in which an academic education prepares one for employment. However, when training for specific vocations, such as medicine, plumbing, electrical work, computer programming, or finance, the same principle of insularity is important. Training for a given profession will best be accomplished in the presence of those who have already acquired the specialist knowledge and skills specific to the job. Commenting upon the British higher education system prior to the introduction of government-backed vocational qualifications, Michael Young suggests that three crucial features were shared by academic and professional/vocational institutions:

> (i) [T]hey provided clear progression routes between lower levels (e.g. A-levels and National Certificate courses) and higher levels (degrees, Higher National Certificates and professional qualifications), (ii) they depended for their validity on the understandings and values shared within different communities of specialists, and (iii) they maintained quality by relying on a combination of established external examinations and trust within the specialist communities.[36]

These established procedures, relationships of trust, and communities of specialists have all been eroded through the logic of making education and training more responsive to "global" conditions. However, this pattern also lights a path for returning both education and training into bounded activities governed by distinct communities of specialists.

Boundaries between different communities

Above, we considered the importance of bounded communities with a given expertise. Here, we will emphasize a different type of community: one that consists of like-minded adults, and their offspring. Such communities can vary in size and geographical distribution, but what binds them together is some common agreement about the values they wish to uphold and pass on to their children. Because humans give meaning to facts and objects, their significance and how we respond to new findings are open to interpretation. In a democracy, the meaning of knowledge will always be contested, and different people will have different systems of meaning. This does not mean that morality is relative: rather that we tolerate different opinions, even as we challenge them, and we respect the rights of parents to bring up their children as they see fit.

Here, it is important to recognize that education is tied to a sense of who we are and what we believe in.[37] It is tied to communities of people who share something in common: aspirations, culture, values, or beliefs such as a common faith in humanity. Historically, this has allowed people of different religions to educate their children in their religious beliefs as well subject knowledge. And, under the international system of nation states, education has frequently emphasized national culture, national traditions, and a national perspective on the world. For a given community, the significance of education is the maintenance of the community, its beliefs, its ideals, but also its evolution. When adults educate children, they are seeking "to prepare them in advance for the task of renewing a common world. "[38]

This is the point emphasized by E. D. Hirsch in his book *The Making of Americans*. He notes that a principal aim of public schools was to teach children about the meaning of America, which is why it was often cited in school documentation. The following early nineteenth-century extract from *The Common School System of the State of New York* by Samuel Randall is one such example:

> As men we have the right to adopt religious creeds, and to attempt to influence others to adopt them; but as Americans, as legislators or officials dispensing privileges or immunities among American citizens, we have no right to know one religion from another. The persecuted and wandering Israelite comes here, and he finds no bar in our naturalization laws. The members of the Roman, Greek, or English church equally become citizens. Those adopting every hue of religious faith, every phase of heresy, take their place equally under the banner of the Republic and no ecclesiastical power can snatch even the least of these from under its glorious folds.[39]

A moral framework derived from a community of adults is precisely what is missing in global education. In contrast, international schools serve a particular community which has particular values they wish to uphold. Depending upon the context, parents send their children to international schools for a variety of reasons, but usually it is a conscious decision not to send them to a local school. Instead, they might want them to learn in an international language, to gain qualifications that are internationally recognized, or to value different cultural traditions. In contrast, who is the constituency of adults being served by global education?

The purpose of global education appears to be to remove education from communities of adults and their particular beliefs. This is evident by its rejection of subject knowledge by association with nation-states, and its promotion of diversity while actively discouraging engagement with different ideas and cultures. As we have noted, the values upheld by global educators—nonjudgmental tolerance, participation, diversity, social justice—lack moral and substantive content precisely because they are not tied to a constituency that has a common sense of meaning and interests. As Furedi suggests, without clarifying what one is participating in, the value of participation takes on the form of a platitude.[40]

The failure to engage with different perspectives, or to be critical of different versions of knowledge or cultural beliefs and practices, means avoiding questions of morality and truth. With global ethics we found that the primary source of moral authority in global education is the self. Of course, engagement with the self cannot provide a moral basis for a society, and nor can it result in education. In order to educate, one has to have something meaningful to communicate to the next generation. When teachers believe in their subjects and the values upheld by the community, they are more likely to communicate these with an infectious passion; only when this happens do children receive an education.

Conclusion

This chapter has demonstrated how bounding education is necessary to give it moral worth. We began with the observation that making distinctions is the basis of knowledge. It is through knowledge that we begin to understand the physical and human worlds, and can also make sense of our own lives. It is through knowledge that we obtain and maintain our humanity. Passing on knowledge and meaning to children is the process of education. The moral worth of this knowledge and its meaning has social origins: it derives from communities of disciplinary specialists and communities of like-minded adults. If these bonds and boundaries are undermined, as they are with global education, teachers will struggle to educate children and students.

However, there is one important caveat to add to the bounding necessary for education. "Boundaries are the condition both for the constitution of sense and for the transcendence of boundaries," proclaims Muller.[41] There are times when certain boundaries need to be crossed and we must recognize that some boundaries are porous. For instance, interdisciplinary research or teaching can be very enlightening as disciplines approach knowledge from their unique perspectives. In reality, the boundary between children and adults is not a fixed, clear line; there are times we ask mature children to take on the responsibilities of adults, such as minding younger children.

Transcending boundaries can extend meaning beyond them. In reality, no culture is entirely exclusive; all cultures have borrowed from others. Yet before we can begin to transcend their boundaries, we must understand what makes each culture unique. The transcendence of boundaries is also a precondition for universalism, in both knowledge and morality. But first we must learn where the lines are and the significance of each, so that we can evaluate them. In the words of Muller: "To cross the line without knowing it is to be at the mercy of the power inscribed in the line." [42] The question is how to cross and why?

Notes

1   Sommel cited in Muller (2000) p. 75.
2   Young (2008) p. xvi.
3   Muller (2000).
4   Fish (2008) p. 13.
5   Ibid. p. 27.
6   Ibid. p. 30.
7   Furedi (2009) p. 120.
8   Pike (2000) p. 70.
9   Kumar (1997) p. 100.
10   Silas Wright, cited in Hirsch (2009) p. 7.
11   Putnam (2001).
12   Laïdi (1998).
13   Hirsch (2009) p. 31.
14   Arendt (1968) p. 183.

15 Ibid. p. 183.

16 Muller (2000); Young (2008).

17 Young (2008) p. 41.

18 Muller (2000) p. 79.

19 Young (2008) p. 42.

20 Pike and Selby (2000) p. 54.

21 Ibid. p. 55.

22 Young (2008) p. 9.

23 Muller (2000) p. 152.

24 Ibid. p. 152.

25 Williams, cited in Young (2008) p. xviii.

26 For example, see Ecclestone and Hayes (2009); Young (2008).

27 Ecclestone and Hayes (2009) p. 143.

28 Reported by Muller (2000) p. 67.

29 Ibid. p. 67.

30 Gibbons *et al.* (1994).

31 Muller (2000) p. 51.

32 See Wolf (2002); Senechal (2010).

33 Ecclestone and Hayes (2009).

34 Young (2008) p. 156.

35 See Wolf (2002).

36 Young (2008) p. 142.

37 Young (2008) p. xvi.

38 Arendt (1968) p. 193.

39 Samuel S. Randall, *The Common School System of the State of New York*, cited in Hirsch (2009) p. 73.

40 Furedi (2009) p. 117.

41 Muller (2000) p. 76.

42 Ibid. p. 71.

CONCLUSION:
AVOIDING
RESPONSIBILITY FOR
EDUCATION

This book has shown how contemporary Anglo-American culture has employed the term global to break down boundaries and redefine the meaning of education. The growing popularity of the many guises and themes of global education stems from a loss of belief in knowledge and moral systems of meaning, expressing the decline of nation building and other projects of social transformation. The failure of both elites and alternative social movements to provide a vision for advancing society means that collectively we are unsure about what to teach the next generation. We don't need any more surveys or reports to know that public schools in both the US and England are, in general, failing to educate children.[1] From the pragmatic and managerial policies of Bloomberg's administration in New York, and the social engineering policies of New Labour, it is also clear that governments across the Atlantic have been at a loss as to how to solve the problem.

Global education needs to be understood in this context of lost leadership. Conceptually and practically, making education global has been a way of enabling others to take over the curriculum and fill the moral void with their own agendas. This has included corporations who want to use education to train workers, progressive educators who see education as a therapeutic exploration of the inner self, academics who want to nurture global citizens informed by postmodern values, and nonprofit organizations who want children to embrace their political agenda of human rights, sustainable development, or saving the environment. This is not just a case of broadening the discussion about the purpose of education, but many of these actors have been coopted to write standards, policy documents, teaching materials, and sometimes given responsibility for managing schools or training teachers. In the case of New York, business leaders have been asked to train school principals, and one (Catherine Black) was placed incharge of the largest school system in America. In England, the Department for International Development has funded global education programs and training offered by nonprofits. Nonprofits were also instrumental in shaping the content of key government policy documents: the most significant example being Oxfam's *Curriculum for Global Citizenship*, which was incorporated into the citizenship national curriculum, launched in 2000.[2]

We should therefore understand global education in a similar vein to America's charter schools and England's academies. The government has been farming out responsibility for education to those who claim to have a plan. Where the analogy breaks down is that charter schools and academies do not necessarily have alternative agendas for education—although charter schools have been a key means through which philanthropists such as Bill Gates have imported business management practices into schools. The colonization of education is not some deliberate ploy to destroy schools or deny children an education. Rather, as Graham Pike proposes, we should view global education as "in pursuit of meaning."[3] This search takes place not within our society, not in our systems of belief, but elsewhere: outside of communities, outside of knowledge, outside of adults, outside of our society, outside of education.

Global knowledge, global skills, and global values cannot resolve the crisis of meaning in our societies because they are not asking the important questions about what we stand for and which knowledge we should teach children. Global ethics circumvent a discussion about the moral basis for our lives. Values of diversity, tolerance, empathy, participation or being a "global citizen" all avoid asking difficult questions about which ideas and cultural practices are better than others. This is the "whatever" approach to morality. The values inherent to the global approach expressly seek to steer children away from communities with a moral framework. They discourage culturally rooted learning and claims to exceptionalism. This is why we have witnessed clashes between teachers and parents in some parts of the US: the parents see "international values" as in conflict with their American values.[4] Advocates of global ethics seek identity and an education (which they present as synonymous) through others, other cultures or through nature. The message for children is that they should regulate their lives in response to global processes (economic, environmental, and cultural) beyond their control.

In the previous chapter, we noted that questions about "what it is to be educated or to educate someone" are "philosophical and political questions about who we are and what we value."[5] Therefore, without a *telos*, or at least a discussion about what binds us together and what our collective aspirations are, it becomes very difficult to know what knowledge to pass on to our children. It is this confusion which is the heart of the problem with education in Anglo-American culture. The problem lies not with some fundamentally different needs of children in a "global world," but rather with adults who are avoiding a discussion about the future direction of society, and fundamental questions about what it means to be human. Global education contributes to the problem by offering a rationale for schooling that circumvents the discussion of these problems in the adult world.

Thus, the global perspective is one which undermines our human potential. In blurring the lines between mind and reality, between nature and culture, between knowledge and experience, between education and political activism, or by equating education with preparation for labor, advocates fail to clarify our human virtues. Both the economic skills and global ethics approach to global education reject knowledge as a path to making sense of the world and acting upon it. Without knowledge and understanding of our world, without a discussion of human potential, we are lesser beings; merely practical creatures who gaze inward at ourselves instead of out into the world with intent.

Fortunately, not everybody has lost faith in knowledge and morality. There is a yearning for common culture, a pining for systems of meaning, and an aspiration to pass on knowledge and real skills to children. Two examples of this are E. D. Hirsch's *Core Knowledge Sequence*[6] and the national curriculum review that is, at the time of writing, being undertaken by the Conservative/Liberal Democrat Coalition government in the UK.[7] The former is now used by over one thousand schools, while the latter is intent on "refocusing on the core subject knowledge."[8] This is not to endorse either initiative or the rationale behind them: it is merely to note that in both instances we find people who are engaged in a discussion of what knowledge we value and want to pass on to our children, which is simultaneously a discussion about what we believe in as a society. However, in both examples the intrinsic rationale for education is inadequately developed. In order to resuscitate education we need to clarify the educative value of knowledge itself, rather than tying it to instrumental purpose.

Another example of where people still value academic knowledge is independent schools. Historically, such schools have been run by individuals committed to high standards of education. It is their place outside of the state sector that has sheltered them from global education initiatives, and they are more resistant to allowing their curriculum to be determined by Oxfam or Bill Gates. But as a part of society, these institutions are not immune to wider cultural trends either.

Such examples provide hope that things can be different. If others in American and English societies add their voices to the debate about the meaning of education and which knowledge is of value, *the false promise of global learning* may find itself exposed, and education can be placed back in the hands of those responsible for its delivery: teachers, with the support of communities.

Notes

1 See Furedi (2009); Ravitch (2010).

2 Oxfam (1997).

3 Pike (2000) p. 64.

4 Education News "Protestors Call IB Program un-American. Is it?" 2010. Accessed: http://www.educationnews.org/ednews_today/91338.html

5 Young (2008) p. xvi.

6 Core Knowledge Foundation (2010) *Core Knowledge Sequence: Content and Skill Guidelines for Grades K-8*. Charlottesville, VA: Core Knowledge Foundation.

7 Disclosure: at the request of the Minister for Schools, I have submitted a geography curriculum as a contribution to the national curriculum review.

8 Department for Education (2010) p. 10.

SELECTED BIBLIOGRAPHY

Advisory Group on Citizenship (1998) *Education for Citizenship and the Teaching of Democracy in Schools: Final Report of the Advisory Group on Citizenship*. London: Qualifications and Curriculum Authority.

Anderson, L. (1979) *Schooling and Citizenship in a Global Age: An Exploration of the Meaning and Significance of Global Education*. Bloomington, IN: Mid-American Program for Global Perspectives in Education, Social Studies Development Center.

Arendt, H. (2006 [1968]) *Between Past and Future* (with an introduction by J. Kohn). New York: Penguin.

Arum, R. and Roksa, R. (2011) *Academically Adrift: Limited Learning on College Campuses*. Chicago, IL: University of Chicago Press.

Banks, D. (2002) 'What is the State of Human Rights Education in K-12 Schools in the United States in 2000? A Preliminary Look at the National Survey of Human Rights Education', Paper presented at the Annual Meeting of the *American Educational Research Association* (Seattle, WA, April 10–14, 2001).

Baughen, M., Baughen, B., Glackin, M., Hopper, G. and Inman, S. (2006) *Making a Difference: Global Citizenship in Initial Teacher Training*, report of the Global Citizenship Initial Teacher Training Scheme developed by London and the South East Regions Global Dimension and the Centre for Cross Curricular Initiatives, London South Bank University. London: London South Bank University.

Bayliss, V. (1999) *Opening Minds: Education for the 21st Century*. London: Royal Society for the Encouragement of the Arts.

Becker, J. (1979) (ed.) *Schooling for a Global Age*. New York: McGraw-Hill.

—(1982) 'Goals for Global Education', *Theory into Practice*, 21(3), 228–33.

—(1991) 'Curriculum Considerations in Global Studies' in K. Tye (ed.) *Global Education: From Thought to Action*. Alexandria, VA: Association for Supervision of Curriculum Development.

Bourn, D. and Hunt, F. (2011) *Global Dimension in Secondary Schools*. London: Development Education Research Center: Research Paper #1. Accessed: http://www.oecd.org/dataoecd/56/53/47522080.pdf

British Council (2011) 'International School Award'. Accessed: http://www.britishcouncil.org/learning-international-school-award.htm

Bryan, J. (2004) 'FE Cannot Save the Economy' in D. Hayes (ed.) *The RoutledgeFalmer Guide to Key Debates in Education*. London: RoutledgeFalmer.

Buergenthal, T. and Torney, J. (1976) *International Human Rights and International Education*. Washington, D.C.: US National Commission for UNESCO.

Bunnell, T. (2008) 'The International Baccalaureate in England and Wales: The Alternative Paths for the Future', *Curriculum Journal*, 19(3), 151–60.

Burack, J. (2003) 'The Student, the World, and the Global Education Ideology' in J. Leming, L. Ellington & K. Porter-Magee (eds.) *Where Did the Social Studies Go Wrong?* Washington, D.C.: Thomas B Fordham Institute.

Byrd, S., Ellington, L., Gross, P., Jago, C. and Stern, S. (2007) *Advanced Placement and International Baccalaureate: Do They Deserve Gold Star Status?* Washington, D.C.: Thomas B. Fordham Institute.

Cambridge, J. and Thompson, J. (2004) 'Internationalism and Globalization as Context for International Education', *Compare*, 34(2), 161–75.

Camicia, S. and Saavedra, M. (2009) 'A New Social Studies Curriculum for a New Generation of Citizenship', *Journal of Children's Rights*, 17, 501–17.

Castells, M. (1996) *The Information Age: Economy, Society and Culture* (3 vols.). Oxford: Blackwell.

Center for International Understanding (2006) *North Carolina in the World: Preparing North Carolina Teachers for an Interconnected World*. The Center for International Understanding: University of North Carolina.

Central Bureau/Development Education Association (2000) *A Framework for the International Dimension for Schools in England*. London: the Central Bureau/Development Education Association.

Chandler, D. (2002) *From Kosovo to Kabul: Human Rights and International Intervention*. London: Pluto Press.

—(2009) *Hollow Hegemony: Rethinking Global Politics, Power and Resistance*. London: Macmillan.

Chevalier, A. and Lindley, J. (2009) 'Over-education and the Skills of UK Graduates', *Journal of the Royal Statistical Society*, 172(2), 307–37.

Council of Chief State School Officers & the National Governors Association (2010) *Common Core State Standards* for English Language Arts & Literacy in History/Social Studies, Science, and Technical Subjects. Accessed: http://www.corestandards.org/assets/CCSSI_ELA%20Standards.pdf

Cox, C. and Scruton, R. (1984) *Peace Studies: A Critical Survey*. London: Institute for European Defence and Strategic Studies.

CREDO (2009) *Multiple Choice: Charter School Performance in Sixteen States*. Center for Research on Educational Outcomes, Stanford University. Accessed: http://credo.stanford.edu/reports/MULTIPLE_CHOICE_CREDO.pdf

Crews, R. (1989) 'A Values Based Approach to Peace Studies' in D. Thomas & M. Klare (eds.) *Peace and World Order Studies: A Curriculum Guide*. Boulder, CO: Westview Press.

Critchley, M. and Unwin, R. (2008) *Whole-School Development and the Global Dimension/Global Citizenship: Capturing Models of Practice across the UK*. Sheffield: Development Education Center South Yorkshire.

Czarra, F. (2003) 'Global Education Checklist for Teachers, Schools, School Systems and State Education Agencies', *Occasional Papers from the American Forum for Global Education*, 173.

Department for Education (2010) *The Importance of Teaching*. London: Department for Education.

Department for Education and Employment (1998) *The Learning Age: A Renaissance for a New Britain* (summary). London: Department for Education and Employment.

Department for Education and Skills (2002) *Languages for All: Languages for Life: A Strategy for England*. Accessed: https://www.education.gov.uk/publications/eOrderingDownload/DfESLanguagesStrategy.pdf

—(2004) *Putting the World into World-Class Education: An International Strategy for Education, Skills and Children's Services*. London: Department for Education and Skills.

—(2005) *Excellence and Enjoyment: Social and Emotional Aspects of Learning (Primary National Strategy)*. Accessed: https://www.education.gov.uk/publications/eOrderingDownload/DFES0110200MIG2122.pdf

Department for Education and Skills/Department for International Development (2005) *Developing the Global Dimension in the Curriculum*. London: Department for International Development, Department for Education and Skills, Development Education Association, Qualifications and Curriculum Authority, Sure Start, & the British Council.

Department for International Development (2007) *The World Classroom: Developing Global Partnerships in Education*. London: Department for International Development.

Development Education Association (2004) *Geography: The Global Dimension* (Key Stage 3). London: DEA.

Dicken, P. (2003) *Global Shift: Reshaping the Global Economic Map in the 21st Century*. New York: Guildford Press.

Dowling, P. (1993) 'Mathematics, Theoretical "Totems": A Sociological Language for Educational Practice' in C. Julie, D. Angelis & Z. Davis (eds.) *Curriculum Reconstruction for a Society in Transition*, Proceedings of the Political Dimensions of Mathematics Education, Second International Conference, Johannesburg.

Duffield, M. (2001) *Global Governance and the New Wars: The Merger of Development and Security*. New York: Zed Books.

Ecclestone, K. and Hayes, D. (2009) *The Dangerous Rise of Therapeutic Education*. London: Routledge.

Ferve, R. W. (2000) *The Demoralization of Western Culture: Social Theory and the Dilemmas of Modern Living*. New York: Continuum.

Fish, S. (2008) *Save the World on Your Own Time*. New York: Oxford University Press.

Fisher, S. (1985) *World Studies 8–13: A Teacher's Handbook*. Edinburgh: Oliver & Boyd.

Frayn, N. (2010) *Bloomberg's Impoverished Vision for Education: The Contemporary Politics of Pragmatism*. Unpublished paper.

Fukuyama, F. (1992) *The End of History and the Last Man*. London: Hamish Hamilton.

Furedi, F. (2009) *Wasted: Why Education is Not Educating*. London: Continuum.

—(2011) *On Tolerance: A Defense of Moral Independence*. London: Continuum.

Gärdenfors, P. (2007) 'Understanding Cultural Patterns' in M. Suárez-Orozoco (ed.) *Learning in the Global Era: International Perspectives on Globalization and Education*. Berkley, LA: California University Press, pp. 67–84.

Garforth, H., Hopper, L., Lowe, B. and Robinson, L. (2006) *Growing up Global: Early Years Global Education Handbook*. Reading, UK: Reading International Solidarity Center.

Gaudelli, W. (2003) *World Class: Teaching and Learning in Global Times*. Mahwah, NJ: Lawrence Erlbaum Associates.

Gaudelli, W. and Fernekes, W. (2004) 'Teaching About Global Human Rights for Global Citizenship: Action Research in the Social Studies Curriculum', *The Social Studies* 95(1), 16–26.

Gibbons, M., Limoges, C., Nowotny, H., Schwartzman, S., Scott, P. and Trow, M. (1994) *The New Production of Knowledge*. London: Sage.

Gourevitch, A. (2007) 'National Insecurities: The New Politics of American National Self-Interest' in J. Bickerton, P. Cunliffe & A. Gourevitch (eds.) *Politics without Sovereignty: A Critique of Contemporary International Relations*. London: University College of London Press.

Graves, J. (2002) 'Developing a Global Dimension in the Curriculum,' *The Curriculum Journal*, 13(3), 303–11.

Gutek, G. (1993) *American Education in a Global Society: Internationalizing Teacher Education*. Loyola University Chicago, IL: Waveland Press.

Haipt, M. (1980) *Multicultural and Global Education: Relationships and Possibilities*. World Education Monograph Series Number Three. Connecticut University, Storrs: World Education Project.

Hanvey, R. (2004 [1976]) *An Attainable Global Perspective*, republished by the American Forum for Global Education. Accessed: http://www. globaled.org/an_att_glob_persp_04_11_29.pdf

Harding, H. (2005) 'Creating Curiosity about International Affairs', *The State Education Standard*, 6(1), 8–11.

Harwood, D. (1995) 'The Pedagogy of the World Studies 8–13 Project: The Influence of the Presence/Absence of the Teacher upon Primary Children's Collaborative Group Work', *British Educational Research Journal*, 21(5), 587–611.

Hayden, M. (2006) *Introduction to International Education: International Schools and Their Communities*. London: Sage.

Hayden, M., Thompson, J. and Levy, J. (2007) (eds.) *The SAGE Handbook of Research in International Education*. London: Sage.

Heater, D. (1982) 'Education for International Understanding: A View from Britain', *Theory into Practice*, 21(3), 218–23.

Heilman, E. (2009) 'Terrains of Global and Multicultural Education: What is Distinctive, Contested, and Shared?' in T. F. Kirkwood-Tucker (ed.) *Visions in Global Education*. New York: Peter Lang, pp. 25–46.

Hicks, D. (2003) 'Thirty Years of Global Education: What Have we Learnt?' *Educational Review*, 44(3), 265–75.

—(2007a) 'Responding to the World' in D. Hicks & C. Holden (eds.) *Teaching the Global Dimension: Key Principles and Effective Practices*. London: Routledge, pp. 3–13.

—(2007b) 'Principles and Precedents' in D. Hicks & C. Holden (eds.) *Teaching the Global Dimension*. London: Routledge, pp. 14–30.

Hirsch, E. D. (2006) *The Knowledge Deficit: Closing the Shocking Education Gap for American Children*. Boston, MA: Houghton Mifflin.

—(2009) *The Making of Americans: Democracy and Our Schools*. New Haven, CT: Yale University Press.

Hirst, P. and Thompson, G. (1998) *Globalization in Question* (2nd edition). Malden, MA: Polity.

Holden, C. (2000) 'Learning for Democracy: From World Studies to Global Citizenship', *Theory into Practice*, 39(2), 74–80.

Hunter, J. (2001) *The Death of Character: Moral Education in an Age Without Good or Evil*. New York: Basic Books.

Huntington, S. (2004) *Who Are We? Challenges to America's National Identity*. New York: Simon and Schuster.

Hyle, J. and McCarthy, J. (2003) 'International Education and Teacher Preparation in the US', Paper presented at the Duke University conference *Global Challenges and US Higher Education: National Needs and Policy Implications*.

Internationalization Strategic Planning Group (2005) *Global Education Strategic Plan*. Fairleigh Dickinson University. Accessed: http://view.fdu.edu/files/globedstratplan051107.pdf

Isin, E. and Turner, B. (2002) (eds.) *Handbook of Citizenship Studies*. Thousand Oaks, CA: Sage.

Jones, S. and Murphy, M. (1962) *Geography and World Affairs*. HM Rand.

Kaldor, M. (2005) 'The Idea of Global Civil Society' in B. Gideon & D. Chandler (eds.) *Global Civil Society: Contested Futures*. London: Routledge, pp. 103–13.

Kane, M., Berryman, S., Goslin, D. and Meltzer, A. (1990) *The Secretary's Commission on Achieving the Necessary Skills: Identifying and Describing the Skills Required by Work*. Prepared for US Department of Labor. Accessed: http://wdr.doleta.gov/SCANS/idsrw/idsrw.pdf

Klein, M. and Tye, K. (1979) 'Curriculum Planning for World-Centered Schools' in J. Becker (ed.) *Schooling for a Global Age*. New York: McGraw-Hill.

Kolodziej, E. (2005) *Plotting an Intellectual Jailbreak: Rationale for Globalizing the Campus and University*, Occasional Paper, Center for Global Studies, University of Illinois at Urbana-Champaign.

Kronman, A. (2007) *Education's End: Why our Colleges and Universities have Given up on the Meaning of Life*. New Haven, CT: Yale University Press.

Kumar, C. (1997) 'The Post-Modern Condition' in A. H. Halsey, H. Lauder, P. Brown & A. S. Wells (eds.) *Education: Culture, Economy, Society*. Oxford: Oxford University Press, pp. 96–112.

Laïdi, Z. (1998) *A World Without Meaning: The Crisis of Meaning in International Politics*. New York: Routledge.

Lawes, S. (2007) 'Foreign Languages Without Tears?' in R. Whelan (ed.) *The Corruption of the Curriculum*. London: CIVITAS, pp. 86–97.

Ledda, M. (2007) 'English as a Dialect' in R. Whelan (ed.) *The Corruption of the Curriculum*. London: CIVITAS, pp. 11–27.

Levine, M. (2005) *Putting the World into Our Classrooms*, Policy Brief April 2005, Progressive Policy Institute.

Levy, F. and Murnane, R. (2007) 'How Computerized Work and Globalization Shape Human Skills Demands' in M. Suárez-Orozoco (ed.) *Learning in the Global Era: International Perspectives on Globalization and Education*. Berkley, LA: California University Press, pp. 158–74.

Librera, W., Ten Eyck, R., Doolan, J., Morse, L. and Jensen, J. (2005) *New Jersey International Education Summit Report*. http://www.state.nj.us/education/international/summit/report.pdf

Lidstone, J. and Stoltman, J. P. (2002) 'International Understanding and Geographical Education', *International Research in Geographical and Environmental Education*, 11(4), 309–12.

Machon, P. and Walkington, H. (2000) 'Citizenship: The Role of Geography?' in A. Kent (ed.) *Reflective Practice in Geography Teaching*. London: Paul Chapman Publishing, pp. 179–91.

Malik, K. (2008) *Strange Fruit: Why Both Sides are Wrong in the Race Debate*. Oxford: Oneworld.

Marsden, M. (1989) 'All in a Good Cause: Geography, History and the Politicization of the Curriculum in Nineteenth and Twentieth Century England', *Journal of Curriculum Studies*, 21(6), 509–26.

Marshall, H. (2005) 'Developing the Global Gaze in Citizenship Education: Exploring the Perspective of Global Education NGO Workers in England', *International Journal of Citizenship and Teacher Education*, 1(2), 76–92.

Marshall, H. and Arnot, M. (2009) 'Globalizing the School Curriculum: Gender, EFA and Global Citizenship Education', *Research Consortium on Educational Outcomes and Poverty*, Working Paper #17.

Mayhew, R. (2000) *Enlightenment Geography: The Political Languages of British Geography 1650–1850*. New York: St. Martin's Press.

McGovern, C. (2007) 'The New History Boys' in R. Whelan (ed.) *The Corruption of the Curriculum*. London: CIVITAS, pp. 58–85.

Meadows, D. H., Meadows, D. L., Randers, J. and Behrens, III W. (1972) *The Limits to Growth: A Report for the Club of Rome's Project on the Predicament of Mankind*. New York: Universe Books.

Merryfield, M. M. (1993) 'Reflective Practice in Teacher Education in Global Perspectives: Strategies for Teacher Educators', *Theory into Practice*, 32(1), 27–32.

Midgley, M. (2007) *Earthly Realism: The Meaning of Gaia*. Exeter: Imprint Academic.

Morgan, A. (2006) 'Teaching Geography for a Sustainable Future' in D. Balderstone (ed.) *Secondary Geography Handbook*. Sheffield: Geographical Association.

Morris, D. (1979) 'Elementary School Programs' in J. Becker (ed.) *Schooling for a Global Age*. New York: McGraw-Hill.

Mullar, J. (2000) *Reclaiming Knowledge: Social Theory, Curriculum and Education Policy*. London: Routledge/Falmer.

National Center on Education and the Economy (2007) *Tough Choices Tough Times: The Report of the New Commission on the Skills of the American Workforce*. San Francisco, CA: Jossey-Bass.

National Governors Association (1989) *America in Transition: The International Frontier*, Report of the Task Force on International Education. Washington, D.C.: National Governors Association.

New Jersey Department of Education (2006) *New Jersey Core Curriculum Content Standards for Social Studies*. New Jersey: Department of Education.

— (2009) *Revised Core Curriculum Content Standards Posted for Review*. Accessed: http://www.state.nj.us/education/news/2009/0206cccs.htm

Noddings, N. (2005) 'Global Citizenship: Promises and Problems' in N. Noddings (ed.) *Educating Citizens for Global Awareness*. New York: Teachers College, pp. 1–21.

Nolan, J. (1998) *The Therapeutic State: Justifying Government at Century's End*. New York: New York University Press.

Office of Education (1979) *US Commissioner of Education Task Force on Global Education: Report with Recommendations*. Washington, D.C.: Office of Education.

Office for Standards in Education (2011) *Geography: Learning to make a world of difference*. London: OFSTED.

Osterhammel, J. and Peterson, N. (2005) *Globalization: A Short History*. Princeton, NJ: Princeton University Press.

Oxfam (1997) *Curriculum for Global Citizenship, Oxfam Development Educational Programme*. Oxford: Oxfam.

— (2006) *Education for Global Citizenship: A Guide for Schools*. Accessed: http://www.oxfam.org.uk/education/gc/files/education_for_global_citizenship_a_guide_for_schools.pdf

Parker (2008) 'International Education: What's in a Name?' *Phi Delta Kappa*, 90(3), 196–202.

Partnership for 21st Century Skills (2003) *Learning for the 21st Century: A Report and Mile Guide for 21st Century Skills*. Accessed: http://www.p21.org/images/stories/otherdocs/p21up_Report.pdf

Payne, J. (2000) 'The Unbearable Lightness of Skill: The Changing Meaning of Skill in the UK Policy Discourses and Some Implications for Education and Training', *Journal of Education Policy*, 15(3), 353–69.

Pigozzi, M. J. (2006) 'A UNESCO View of Global Citizenship Education', *Educational Review*, 58(1), 1–4.

Pike, G. (2000) 'Global Education and National Identity: In Pursuit of Meaning', *Theory into Practice*, 39(2), 64–73.

Pike, G. and Selby, D. (1988) *Global Teacher, Global Learner*. London: Hodder and Stoughton.

—(2000) *In the Global Classroom*. Toronto, Canada: Pippin.

—(2001) *In the Global Classroom 2*. Toronto, Ontario: Pippin.

Pring, R. (1995) *Closing the Gap: Liberal Education and Vocational Preparation*. London: Hodder and Stoughton.

Putnam, R. (2000) *Bowling Alone: The Collapse and Revival of American Community*. New York: Simon & Schuster.

Ravitch, D. (2010a) *The Life and Death of the Great American School System: How Testing and Choice Are Undermining Education*. New York: Basic Books.

—(2010b) 'A Century of Skills Movements', *American Educator*, 34(1), Spring, 12–13.

Reading International Solidarity Center (2008) *All You Need for a Sustainability Assembly*. UK: Reading International Solidarity Center.

Rearden, B. (1989) 'Pedagogical Approaches to Peace Studies' in D. Thomas & M. Klare (eds.) *Peace and World Order Studies: A Curriculum Guide*. Boulder, CO: Westview Press.

Rischard, J. F. (2002) *High Noon: 20 Global Problems and 20 Years to Solve Them*. New York: Basic Books.

Rosenberg, J. (2000) *The Follies of Globalisation Theory*. London: Verso.

Sassens, S. (2002) 'Towards Post-national and Denationalized Citizenship' in E. Isin & B. Turner (eds.) *Handbook of Citizenship Studies*. Thousand Oaks, CA: Sage.

Schukar, R. (1993) 'Controversy in Global Education: Lessons for Teacher Educators', *Theory into Practice*, 32(1), 52–7.

Selby, D. (2000) 'A Darker Shade of Green: The Importance of Ecological Thinking in Global Education and School Reform', *Theory into Practice*, 39(2), 88–96.

Senechal, D. (2010) 'The Most Daring Education Reform of All', *American Educator*, 34(1), (Spring), 4–16.

Standish, A. (2009) *Global Perspectives in the Geography Curriculum: Reviewing the Moral Case for Geography*. London: Routledge.

Stapp, W. B., Bennett, D., William Bryan, J., Fulton, J., MacGregor, J., Nowak, P., Swan, J., Wall, R., and Havlick, S. (1969) 'The Concept of Environmental Education', *The Journal of Environmental Education*, 1(1), 30–1.

Stephenson, C. (1989) 'The Evolution of Peace Studies' in D. Thomas & M. Klare (eds.) *Peace and World Order Studies: A Curriculum Guide*. Boulder, CO: Westview Press.

Sylvester, R. (2007) 'Historical Resources for Research in International Education (1851–1950)' in M. Hayden, J. Tompson & J. Levy (eds.) *Sage Handbook of Research in International Education*. London: Sage, pp. 11–24.

Taba, H. and Van Til, W. (1945) *Democratic Human Relations: Promising Practices in Intergroup and Intercultural Education in the Social Studies. Sixteenth Yearbook of the National Council of Social Studies.* Washington, D.C.

Tye, K. (1991) (ed.) *Global Education: From Thought to Action.* Alexandria, Virginia: Association for Supervision of Curriculum Development.

—(2009) 'A History of the Global Education Movement in the United States' in T. F. Kirkwood-Tucker (ed.) *Visions in Global Education: The Globalization of Curriculum and Pedagogy in Teacher Education and Schools.* New York: Peter Lang, pp. 3–24.

United Nations Educational, Scientific and Cultural Organization (1974) *Recommendation Concerning Education for International Understanding, Co-operation and Peace and Education Relating to Human Rights and Fundamental Freedoms.* Adopted by the General Conference at its eighteenth session in Paris: UNESCO.

Wade, P. and Marshall, H., with O'Donnell (2009) *Primary Modern Foreign Languages Longitudinal Survey of Implementation of National Entitlement to Language Learning at Key Stage 2: Final Report.* National Foundation for Educational Research.

White, J. (2004) *Rethinking the School Curriculum: Values, Aims and Purposes.* London: Routledge.

Wiggan, G. and Hutchinson, C. (2009) *Global Issues in Education: Pedagogy, Policy, Practice and the Minority Experience.* New York: Rowan & Littlefield.

Williams, A. (2008) *The Enemies of Progress: The Dangers of Sustainability.* London: Societas.

Williams, J. (2005) 'Skill as a Metaphor: An Analysis of Terminology Used in Success for All and 21st Century Skills', *Journal of Further and Higher Education*, 29(2), 181–90.

Willingham, D. (2007) 'Critical Thinking: Why is it So Hard to Teach?' *American Educator*, Summer, 8–18.

Wisconsin Department of Instruction (2006) *Social Studies Performance Standard C Grade 8.* Accessed: http://dpi.state.wi.us/standards/ssintro.html

Wisconsin Department of Public Instruction (2002) *Planning Curriculum in International Education.* Madison, WI: Wisconsin Department of Public Instruction.

Wolf, A. (2002) *Does Education Matter? Myths about Education and Economic Growth.* London: Penguin.

—(2010) *Review of Vocational Education: The Wolf Report.* Accessed: https://www.education.gov.uk/publications/eOrderingDownload/Wolf-Report.pdf

World Commission On Environment and Development (1987) *Our Common Future*. Oxford: Oxford University Press.

Young, M. (2008) *Bringing Knowledge Back In: From Social Constructivism to Social Realism in the Sociology of Education*. London: Routledge.

Young, M. (with Commins, E.) (2002) *Global Citizenship: The Handbook for Primary Teaching* (Oxfam). Oxford: Chris Kingston Publishing.

Zhang, H. and Foskett, N. (2003) 'Changes in the Subject Matter of Geography Textbooks: 1907–93', *International Research in Geographical and Environmental Education*, 12(4), 312–29.